Frugal Eating
in the New Depression

M. L. Gardner & Daisy E. Lynn

TABLE OF CONTENTS

INTRODUCTION

THIS COOKBOOK FEATURES old-fashioned, simple cooking. You won't find outlandish recipes with exotic ingredients. What you will find is a way to buy basic staples and turn them into a multitude of meals. It is both Molly and Daisy's goal to help people who are struggling in a harsh economy, trying to survive on an ever-shrinking food budget. We aim to help you prepare all of your foods in ways that are interesting and useful, reducing your food waste while saving money. We hope the result of sharing our knowledge, tips, suggestions, and recipes will help people do more with less and reduce the food insecurity in this country.

So make a cup of tea and let Daisy and I introduce ourselves and provide a basic guideline for *Frugal Eating in The New Depression*.

Frugal eating — Basic ingredients meet creativity,
then sprinkled with common sense.

MOLLY'S STORY

AT SOME POINT in time, most of us in the real world have felt that pinch. Something comes up, and we look over the budget and wonder how creative we can get, what to put off, what to pay now, and what can be done without.

On the list of things that can't be done without is food. The cost of food on the rise and with wages stagnant, job losses increasing and an economy—I don't care what they say—that is floundering at best or failing at worse, something has to give.

When it comes time to tighten that belt, it's important to eat well because chances are you're going to have to work harder. Either at two jobs to replace the one that paid well or striking up odd jobs that most often includes labor.

If there is one good thing to come out of this ever so slow train wreck of an economic crisis, it's that there are more entrepreneurs out there than ever. Many people simply must get creative in order to keep going.

This is the new depression. I don't care what talking head says what on TV. Numbers are manipulated a hundred ways from Sunday, and if there is one person out there who hasn't noticed a rise in homelessness and general struggling, I'd like to talk to them. We have so many social programs to mask what's going on today. If the country didn't have social security, welfare, and unemployment, it would look and feel the same if not worse than 1933 at the very height of the depression.

It's number fudging smoke and mirrors. In my opinion, it will get worse.

I first started teaching myself about simple living, scratch cooking, and all the other dollar friendly ways to run a house when we had our own crisis several years ago. We had three small kids. I stayed at home. I wasn't writing books then, and we had no income other than my husband's job, seventy miles away in Seattle.

We were chugging right along like everyone else with dreams and goals. And we were meeting those goals. We had a small but respectable nest egg put away and lived on a budget. And then, all hell broke loose.

When my youngest was just four months old, my oldest fell at school, broke three ribs, each poking a hole in her spleen. She was rushed to Primary Children's Hospital where it was touch and go for three days to see if she would require surgery. They did everything they could to save her spleen, including transfusions and I.V. fluids while the holes clotted. (Then popped out. Then re-clotted. Then popped out again.) At one point, they prepped the O.R. because her blood levels dropped too low and then, by some miracle, her next set of hourly blood work showed a small but promising rise.

Thankfully, my sister had just come into town the day before, and she was able to stay with the younger ones while we went to be with our daughter. My infant son stopped breastfeeding that day and was switched to formula. He was not happy.

Three days after that, my middle child had a previously scheduled surgery on his hip to reverse ball joint damage caused by Perthes disease. A lot of planning had gone into that surgery, and we couldn't reschedule.

After my son had come out of his surgery, we were splitting our time between two hospitals and the baby. The cost to drive sixty miles each way to the hospitals and back plus meals out were starting to add up, as were the co-pays and deductibles on the dual hospital stays. After my husband had missed a week of work, I was starting to get nervous.

Then the urgent care visits started for the youngest. He was not taking to formula well, would scream for hours, and would go days between poos. We spent a lot of money on different formulas to find one that worked and even when my older children emerged from their health crises, we were still trying to figure it out. The formula got me. It was anywhere from twelve to eighteen dollars a can (at the time), and we'd try it for a few days and have to throw it out and try something else.

After a week, my husband had no choice but to go back to work. We had one paid-for vehicle, and thankfully, my children were doing better by that time since I couldn't toggle between hospitals all day. I went in the evening, every other night to see each. That doubled our gas expenses. The savings was dwindling fast.

Then, my son came home. Both legs were cast open so the hip joint would stay still during healing. He now had to use a special rented wheelchair that allowed room for his spread eagle legs.

Soon as we got him settled into a makeshift bedroom downstairs, my oldest came home. She was on strict bed rest for a month. The risk of the clots dislodging was still high if she ran around and played. And my youngest was still having trouble with colic and constipation.

And then—because Murphy's Law wasn't quite done with us—the very last straw reduced me to a crying, sniveling mess. My husband's truck broke down. We had the money to fix it and fix it fast, but it drained the very last of our savings.

I was left thinking, "What now?"

The hospital bills were coming in, and they were nasty. I made arrangements on everything I could, went down to basic cable (and at some point, I turned it off completely because I was too darn busy to watch TV anyway carrying two children to the bathroom every few hours), and we shaved every expense possible. Income that supported us and allowed for some savings was now barely supporting us, allowing for no savings while we tried to pay off the medical debt.

In the span of one week, everything changed with all three of my children having mounting hospital bills and our vehicle sputtering to a stop on the freeway. The end result, after much struggling, was bankruptcy.

Before it got to that, I dove deep into the world of frugality.

The cute tips and tricks that were out there weren't quite enough to get us through our crisis, however. Couponing wasn't the rage back then, but it existed. I was leery of spending ten dollars a week on newspapers with no guarantees I'd end up with more than a freezer of frozen peas and a closet full of shampoo. Couponing rocks—don't get me wrong. But as you'll see in the menus and recipes I've laid out here and still use to this day, coupons don't serve me well outside of shampoo and deodorant.

Shopping sales at the mall? There were no trips to the mall. I had a hard time finding anyone who knew how to get through real lean times with as little misery as possible. Where the hell were all the smart old people anyway? Everyone else was going about their lives, spending money, going on vacation, and I was left in no man's land. So I turned to the generation that defined lean times.

My grandmother's. Unfortunately, she died while I was still pregnant with my youngest, but I remember her stories. I remember a lot of what she told me, and I remember thinking she was superwoman to have lived through all that she had. So I knew her generation was the one I wanted to study.

I got a lot of inspiration from World War II, as well. There were shortages and rationing, and while jobs were plentiful for the war effort, eating well was the bulk of the fight on the home front.

I read biographies, history books, and recipe books. I adapted our entire diet to one of simplicity. (Simplicity that tasted darn good, I might add.)

Our crisis passed, and we went on about our life, eventually resuming saving and rebuilding.

DAISY'S STORY

MY JOURNEY INTO frugal eating didn't begin as dramatically as Molly's, thankfully. Some may disagree with that, but I feel grateful I only had myself to feed when I fully stepped into what is now a way of life for media raised four children on a pretty strict budget. You don't need your calculator to figure out that it's expensive—new sneakers times four certainly costs more than one pair. No, I couldn't purchase school pictures every year, eating out was a real treat for my kids, and there were very few summer vacation events.

I became disabled and unable to work when my children were in grade school. My youngest son was three, and my oldest son was ten. The two girls, the middle two, were six and seven.

Time went on. The kids grew and left home. I became divorced and then remarried thinking this was where I'd spend my golden years in side-by-side rocking chairs. Then, like my co-author, I got blindsided by life.

So when I began a truly frugal way of life in 2012, I had a little knowledge and experience under my belt, but now, thankfully, my children were grown, and I only had myself to feed and take care of.

After just three years of marriage, I found myself starting over alone. I'd just spent nine weeks in a domestic violence shelter, and now, with their help, I was in my own apartment. I had my social security income, monthly food stamps, no bus service, no taxis, and no vehicle. (I live in a very small town in a rural area.) The only way I could get my divorce was to forfeit my car. So now, I had to figure out how to take care of my needs because going back to 'him' was not an option. Statistics show that the average number of times a domestic violence survivor leaves his or her abuser before the final time is five to seven. There are a few reasons for the return to such a horrid life, but financial instability is predominantly why. Not being able to adequately support and house myself caused me to return more than once before my final time. This time, I was determined I'd find a way.

I began simply. Started thinking in terms of what I needed to buy that I could make many things with rather than buying one-use products. So, staples like flour, sugar, dried beans, etc., and I went on from there to add things I could buy in bulk and freeze because I could only get to the store so often... like eggs and cheeses. (Yes, you can freeze eggs.) I then started watching the sale papers for deals and stocked up on canned veggies, canned milk, pasta, etc. And it was only a couple of months before I breathed a sigh of relief knowing I was going to be just fine. In another couple of months, I realized I wasn't *just* fine—I was thriving.

I live on $160 a month in food stamps for just myself, and I eat well. I follow a couple of basic rules: I waste nothing, and I make almost everything from scratch. Yes, it takes more time to cook this way, but most of the time I enjoy cooking. Many of the things I prepare are designed for more than one meal, so less cooking is needed next time, and many recipes have built in seconds for the freezer. I have many meals in my freezer, so anytime I don't want to cook, I can pull one out to thaw and microwave it, and in minutes, I have a great meal. Serving leftovers in a new way is my favorite thing!

Grab a pen and paper and join us. Eating well doesn't have to be expensive, but it does take planning, time, and good old-fashioned *want to*.

THE F WORD

Daisy

THERE ARE 47 million people receiving food stamp benefits today—47 MILLION men, women, and children.

I guarantee you that 46 and a half million of those people never thought they'd be one of the ones receiving food stamps. I'm one of those. I'll bet you don't think you'll ever be a food stamp recipient, either. But you're wrong. Food insecurity can happen to anyone. Job loss can happen to anyone. Health problems can befall anyone. Every person in these precarious economic times should consider themselves just one step away from the nearest food stamp office because you never know when you will be inside it or what situation will bring you there. Don't sneer and think it can't happen to you. Don't believe for one minute that you're above economic ruin or poverty today. I encourage you to learn how to live frugally—our planet's resources matter. Frugality matters on many other levels besides financial. Obesity rates are ridiculous. Morbidity from the diseases caused by obesity is at an all-time high. People should not die from eating themselves to death... and they're dying of malnutrition. So much overfeeding of the wrong foods. This nation's people will see harder times in our near future, and it will be those who can adjust, bend, and adapt who will persevere and survive well through these times. It will be those who are not afraid to work a little harder, to discipline themselves, and to understand that gratification isn't instant as the rest of the world believes. Those willing to not just eat, but to *live* frugally will prevail.

Those who can make something out of nothing will survive the hardest of times. Those who are grateful for and careful with their assets—whether they're food stamps, leftovers, home canning or donated goods—will prosper.

Frugal living and eating aren't for everyone.

Some people are too attached to their crazy ways of spending everything—becoming indebted, wasting money, time, and food in the process—to live a frugal life.

I'm not trying to offend anyone. My purpose is to pull you over to our way of being in the world—but I call it the way I see it. There's entirely too much self-indulgent laziness going on, and while our country's economy slides down the sewer, too many people are drinking a $6 latte and playing games on their iPhones while their kids microwave some frozen cardboard crap for dinner and the house is being foreclosed on. Does that make sense to you? If it does, you don't see the real problem. People, it's about priorities. Let me explain how I see it.

Cooking food and preparing meals are more than just feeding yourself and the ones you care for. It's an act of love, of giving. When you feed someone, you're giving them the stuff life is made of. You're giving them what their body needs to sustain life. That's a pretty awesome thing. If you looked at it that way and treated meal times, meal planning, and meal preparations the same way, wouldn't you want to make a change in the kinds of foods you wanted to serve yourself and your loved ones?

Time is money. Haven't you heard people say that? Well, I think time is love. Time spent giving to your family, your children, is pure love. Combining well-planned meals with shared preparation time with kids pays double time. Your attention means everything to your child. Put your electronic device down and cook a meal with them. They will prosper for it. My kids cooked with me. My grandchildren also cooked with me. It's something you can do with your kids that's free.

Being connected to our families, our food, and our priorities will help all of us to become better people and to make better choices. We may not be so quick to impulse buy expensive items we don't need when we receive joy from talking to a child or seeing our family enjoy a meal we've cooked. Become full, and FULL-filled from simple pleasures rather than material things. Food is meant to fuel your body, not to fill emotional needs. We all need a return to the simple joys of life. I see people so often behind in their mortgage payments and their credit cards maxed, but they are picking up an order at the local pizzeria.

This brings me to my observation that this frugal lifestyle isn't for everyone, as I said in the beginning. You need some "want to" or desire. You have to want to change, want to do things differently, not be afraid of working a bit harder, and then commit to it. You have to know you can eat better and feed your family better than ramen noodles on *whatever* budget or income you have. You can. But it's a choice. Molly and I don't eat fancy or expensive, but we eat well. We eat better than most. I'd rather sit down at night to a good meal KNOWING I have many more meals in my cupboards and freezer to sustain me through the month rather than sit down to a gourmet meal and wonder if I'll have food next week. Far too many people live that way. It's an upside down way to live, but I've seen it. Most people on food stamps eat like kings and queens the first week after they get their food stamps, then struggle the rest of the month to feed themselves. It takes planning and changing a few things to do what Molly and I do. It takes a little work and some small sacrifices... but it's our hope that with this book, a lot of the hard work we've done for you will make your transition to the frugal eating ways somewhat easier.

So—what's the moral of the story? "Want to" gets the job done.

Now, find your "want to" — what's your reason for changing to a frugal lifestyle? Take that reason and keep front and center in your mind and make it the center of all of the changes in your life now. Make this thing the priority and the thing you consider before everything else. Watch how quickly your pantry and cooking changes—then your life and finances!

If you have space—any space, grow some food. Many vegetables grow just fine in containers. As an experiment, this year I grew veggies in repurposed two and a half gallon spring water containers I had from my water. (My town has PFOA in the water and spring water supplied for free.) I grew veggies in large containers before. I wanted to experiment this year to see just how big a container the veggies I prefer *really* need. I have zucchini, cherry tomatoes, beefsteak tomatoes, acorn squash, potatoes, and cucumbers. My zucchini plant succumbed to the 100-degree heat index last week. I got two veggies from it before I lost it. I have a ton of both tomatoes and many cukes for my fall pickles this year. Potatoes are rocking along great too. One big acorn squash so far. All in less than ten feet of space with three bags of soil and a couple of packets of seeds. Total cost was about ten dollars invested. I will gain more than that back in just tomatoes. And no work. Containers equal no weeding. Next year, I will buy containers, bigger ones, and have more return. So, seriously—grow yourself some food. You CAN buy vegetable and fruit seeds with food stamps. Look online and see how to freeze your harvest or learn how to can your vegetables if that interests you. There are savings in growing food. There is security in growing food. Dig up that lawn you hate mowing anyway and grow some food.

THE "W" WORD

Molly

JUST A QUICK word here about grocery stores. I have noticed, over the last few years, Walmart's prices slowly and quietly ticking upward. Of course, the advertising has remained the same. If you want to save money, go to Walmart. Well, I don't think that is the case anymore. Now that they are starting to close stores, I'm wondering if more people have caught on to this.

I rarely, if ever, shop at Walmart. I split my time between Winco, a small mom and pop grocery store, and a Kroger store near me. (Smith's in this neck of the woods.) Of course, the key is to shop sales and store brands. I have found that while Winco consistently has low prices, Kroger has big sales every two weeks, and often the produce is better quality. It's worth the extra three miles I drive. Look around and shop around. It will be worth your time.

STOP WASTING YOUR GROCERY DOLLARS

Daisy

I'M GOING TO be straight with you here and tell you the truth about some things. I see and hear people all the time going to food banks saying they don't have food and their food stamps are gone—that they ran out of those too, and it's only halfway through the month.

That doesn't happen to me. That hasn't ever happened to me.

If it's happening to you or your friends, it's because you're buying the wrong things! I know. I see it in the stores—piles of frozen pizzas and all kinds of junk and snack foods. That crap will make you and your family unhealthy, fat, lazy, and poorer, too.

Buy the things to make homemade pizza. It will cost much less and be much healthier—plus it's an activity you can share with your spouse or kids. Stop putting crap in your shopping cart and in your family's bodies… then watch and see how far your food dollars can go.

I have some recipes for some tasty things to share with you. My homemade chicken tenders are so good, I hope you will stop buying that frozen imitation crap and cook your own. Seriously, read the bag or the box. That is NOT 100% chicken, and since it's not, what exactly is it? Never mind that. Since it's not, WHY ARE YOU EATING IT? If the reason is because it's cheap, we have even cheaper options for you here.

It breaks my heart to hear about people being food insecure, not knowing where their next meal will come from. I have literally cried over it. Just as bad are the children whose diets consist of Ramen noodles because they're cheap and easy to cook. If you're receiving food stamps, be grateful that you've been given a gift and treat it that way by using it with respect. Learn how to shop better, to plan meals, and to cook them. Learn to save and use leftover foods for more meals. I'd like to think if you're reading this book, you've decided you need a little help doing these things, and I'm happy to be able to help. You've come to the right place.

Tonight for dinner, I had barbecue ribs and fried potatoes. I made enough for two dinners. Let me break down for you what these two great BBQ rib dinners cost me:

Ribs: On sale for $1.29/lb. — 2 lbs.
Fried Potatoes: 5# for $1.99 = 40 Cents/lb.
(3 small potatoes = 1lb.)
Plus 1/2 onion leftover in fridge
Bacon Grease: FREE (I fried my potatoes in it.)
MYO* BBQ Sauce: 1 cup = 75 cents
Total cost: $3.73 FOR TWO DINNERS

Total cost for tonight's BBQ RIB DINNER: $1.87

And I have one rib left to snack on later!

Anyone with a small food budget can always use the ways, tips, and recipes Molly and I use.

*Make Your Own

SIMPLICITY

Molly

SIMPLICITY—I JUST love it. I really do. When things got better, I didn't rush back into overspending and rampant consumerism. The week that changed everything for us had changed me forever, and I was hooked on security, not things. I wanted to know that should (if/when) something come flying out of left field again, I'd be able to handle it this time.

That's not to say I don't eat out or buy box food once in a while or sometimes buy expensive food now. I do, on occasion. But I can take my grocery budget down to amounts that would shock you when I have to. Or when I want to for that matter. To this day, I will choose to spend more time in the kitchen so I can put more into savings.

THE FIRST TRUTH ABOUT SIMPLICITY

It isn't always easy. I think people have some link in their brain that connects simplicity to easy. One of my favorite shows is *Mountain Men*. They all live a simple life. And it's hard. Maybe not to them, but to us looking on, what they do to live simple is real work. And so is a simple pantry. If you're going to spend less money on convenience food, then you're going to have to spend more time in the kitchen. This is hard for working moms (and dads), but you can also incorporate once a month cooking and Daisy's ideas for homemade TV dinners to decrease stove time. I won't cover once a month cooking here but do look it up.

THE SECOND TRUTH ABOUT SIMPLICITY

It can be carb heavy. Stretchers, fillers, call them what you want. I call them carbohydrates.

I toggle between a high-carb, low-fat diet, and an ultra-low carb, high-fat diet.

There are arguments for both in the health-boxing arena. When I do high carb, I have more endurance, but a little less quick thinking. Low carb leaves me alert as a hummingbird, but I don't have the stamina to run, much less walk fast. Low carb eases my fibromyalgia symptoms; high carbs help me lift weights. I get food weary on high fat, which is why I toggle between the two.

What I'm laying out is not the "ideal diet" for most people in today's modern, sedentary world. As I said, it's carb heavy and protein and vegetable adequate. If you can afford to boost your menu with anything, fruits and veggies are first. Our grandparents could get away with it because they worked hard. But you're not here to learn the secrets of the perfect diet. You're here to learn how to eat well on very little money.

If you are sensitive to carbs or gain weight easily with carbs, you'll have to be diligent about portion control—which is really hard to do when I get to the fried scones that can be made for pennies. But do your best. Building some kind of muscle is the best way to ward off carb weight. But I'm getting off topic. In the next section, we'll give you examples of how we shop.

SHOPPING WITH DAISY

Daisy

I SHOP ABOUT every two weeks. Occasionally, I pick up sale items in between if they're things I can store and if they're too good to pass up like 88-cent ketchup!

My first trip is meat, produce, anything I need to make something specific, like if I need yeast for bread, cheeses, bulk items, butter, and other dairy.

My second trip consists of things I may be running low on. When I'm down to one, it's time to buy more. Preferably, when I'm down to two, but one, definitely. I have been able to maintain my frugal food budget by never running low on too many things at once. Replacing three items at a time is much less expensive than replacing twelve. That's my best tip for you.

I rarely buy milk. I'm not a milk drinker, but I do eat cereal a few times a month. For this, I use canned evaporated milk. When it's diluted by half with water, it makes whole milk. I also use this for pudding and any other recipes that need milk. It wasn't budget friendly to keep pouring spoiled milk down the drain because I wasn't using it in time.

I buy what is on sale because I am limited to my local store—just one. They have excellent meat sales and vary what is on sale, so I follow the sales and prepare ahead. I buy enough to last until the next sale, or I do not buy it. It's as simple as that. I will not pay $4.99/lb. for boneless chicken breast. I simply cannot afford to. I buy it when it's on sale for $1.99/lb. I buy two big packages and know it will last until it's on sale again. Sometimes, it's buy one, get one free so I will get four, and the following month, I won't have to buy it at all. That's how I restock pantry supplies that may be running low or other things, and I never feel a pinch. See how that works?

Shopping the sales like that means there are months I don't have to buy a number of things, freeing those food dollars for other things I may need or new seasonal things I want to purchase for my pantry. For instance, more salad items in the summer and things like that or more baked bean ingredients in the winter. Shopping ahead frees up some money for me to have more choices.

SHOPPING WITH MOLLY

Molly

I GROCERY SHOP every week. It's what I buy that is rotated out, based on the schedule I've fallen into and what I've chosen to have on the menu. Here's roughly what my weekly trips look like.

Week One: Meat, dairy, fruit, veggies, and small items (canned olives and such)

Week Two: Fruit, veggies.

Week Three: Fruit, veggies, dairy, bulk items (25# flour/sugar/oats, etc.)

Week Four: Fruit, veggies, small items.

So week one, I get all the meat I'll need for the month. I'll go into detail about that shortly. I'll buy fruit and veggies for the week, dairy for two weeks, and any small items I'll need for recipes for the next two weeks.

Week Two is fruit and veggies for the week.

Week Three is fruit, veggies, dairy and bulk items I need to add to—25# flour, sugar, oats, rice, powdered milk, and any of those long-term basic items.

Week Four is fruit and veggies again.

So the cost, averaged for the last several months, breaks down to roughly,

- Week one: $175
- Week two: $50
- Week Three: $175

19

- Week four: $50
- Total: $450

Pretty awesome for a family of four. Even more awesome that everyone enjoys what they are eating.

Now, that said, I have gotten to the point where I have most of my bulk items at home. It's a gradual process to get to this point. Don't beat yourself up if you can't immediately cut your grocery bill in half. While you are working towards that, you can start seeing incremental savings right away by making a few things from scratch instead of buying them.

Take bread for example. We could easily go through one loaf a day of store bought. Even buying the cheap stuff, it would be $30 a month. (Decent bread will cost upwards of $60 a month.) A twenty-five-pound bag of flour costs me nine dollars and makes all our bread plus other things. Even when you factor in the yeast, you are still fifteen dollars (or more) ahead there while eliminating many things besides bread off your list—cakes, cookies, piecrust, thickener for casseroles and mac and cheese, French bread, muffins, hot dog/hamburger buns, just to name a few.

Break down the list of ingredients of a few things you normally buy premade. Start making those at home. Use the savings to buy more ingredients that are basic and expand your options.

THE BASICS

I BUY BASIC ingredients in bulk if I can. Winco, as I said, is great for this. Case lot sales are huge here in Utah, and I take advantage of everyone for my cream soups, canned veggies, and bulk pasta. But a lot can be gathered by shopping sales, too.

Following is a list of groceries you'll need to help you get started. Hopefully, most of them you already have. I'm guessing you might not have them in the quantities needed but don't panic. You can increase stores as you go. Do you have a Winco nearby? I really hope you do. For bulk dry goods, this place has a fantastic self-serve bulk section with everything you could possibly buy in smaller packages. If you don't have a Winco, Walmart now sells some food in bulk, and you can look around for a restaurant supply store. I used one in Tacoma, Washington before I moved nearer to a Winco. Ask around. Just because your local mom and pop grocery doesn't have it, if you are anywhere near a big city, I'm sure you can find big bags and cases of basic ingredients.

If you can gather up enough in bulk, you should only need to buy the basics every few months depending on use. For example, I buy flour monthly but rice every three months. Oats I buy every four months. Based on our use, we've fallen into a pattern that is easy to predict. If you already have these basics, then you're even closer to saving lots of money.

Here's what I consider essential in a pantry at all times:

- Flour
- Sugar
- Baking soda
- Baking powder
- Yeast
- Brown sugar (recipe in Make Your Own section)
- Rice
- Unsweetened cocoa
- Oatmeal
- Mapeline (Maple flavor for syrup, in the spice/flavorings section)
- Oil
- Cornstarch
- Spaghetti
- Elbow noodles

- Spices
- Chicken bouillon powder or soup base
- Beef bouillon powder or soup base
- Powdered sugar
- Poultry gravy
- Beef gravy
- Potatoes
- Potato flakes
- Powdered milk
- Chocolate chips

Once you have these items, what you need to make meals will be reduced to meat, canned goods, some dairy, and produce, and then you will see your grocery bill drastically shrink.

SEASONINGS

Daisy

I'LL ADD A few things to that list that I couldn't survive without.

SEASONINGS

DEFINITELY ESSENTIAL IN my kitchen basics. Garlic powder, cayenne, poultry seasoning, lemon pepper, basil, ground ginger, sage, and cumin. I have more, but these are the basics I recommend having on hand for many uses. No matter what meat or poultry, fish or vegetable you're preparing, if it doesn't taste good, and no one eats it, you haven't saved anything. Money and food are both wasted. Seasonings go a long way to bring out food's flavors, and many can be had very inexpensively.

Once my basics were stocked, I began to compose an area in my kitchen for what I call *extras.* These are things I don't buy monthly but like to have on hand for Justin—as in *Just-in-case*! Just in case the power goes out for a few days, or my stove suddenly breaks, or a bad weather occurrence, whatever scenario comes along that would mean I'd need a short-term alternate food supply that doesn't require cooking or refrigeration. I picked up one or two of these things per shopping trip and put them away in a specific place.

That list includes: peanut butter, cereal, crackers, bottled juices, granola bars, bottled water, canned fruits, instant tea mix, canned tuna, canned spam, pretzels, canned milk, and canned stew. These are the basics that are nutrient rich and will keep energy levels up and a tummy full. Feel free to add whatever else you may like.

While we're talking about shopping lists and basic must haves, I highly recommend a food processor, blender, or something like that, so you can use it for making your own breadcrumbs, grating cheeses, chopping nuts, and making chicken and ham salad, and coleslaw. I have a small electric food chopper I got for ten dollars at a big box store. I also recommend a vacuum food saver—for those of you with one or two person homes, especially. You'll find it invaluable for things you may not use up as quickly as a larger family. Vacuum sealing adds months of freezer time to most foods. This is a good thing for those times when you come across a big sale on something. I got mine on Amazon for $40 and two-50ft rolls of bags for $21. I've not even used up one roll of the bags yet in the three months I've had it. You can also check with your local thrift stores. They may have these items there for just a couple of dollars.

I don't have a specific list I adhere to other than basics. I buy what's on sale and plan my meals around those items. I've always been more partial to chicken than beef or pork, so I eat a lot of chicken. That's all right with me because I prepare it many different ways and never tire of it. The grocery store in my town, Tops, often has buy one, get one free on meats, and every day they have five for $19.99. These smaller packages still save me money, and I can make them into more than one meal per package, so I end up with ten plus meals of meat for my twenty dollars.

My basics list is identical to Molly's... other than, as I said earlier, the seasonings, and I don't buy milk. I also don't buy the dry milk that Molly buys, just as a personal preference. I don't like it. I listed elsewhere my use of canned evaporated milk instead. Molly has a family. I only have myself, so our lists and needs are going to differ, as are yours.

My local grocery store, Tops, often has whole pork tenderloins buy one, get one free. I pay about $18.00 for two. THAT is one good deal. I always buy them, and I've learned to do quite a bit with them. I get about eight dinners and a lunch or two from those two tenderloins. That's about two dollars per meal. FOR PORK TENDERLOIN. If you find your local store or a store in your area has something you like really cheap, find as many ways as you can to cook and enjoy it—and stock up. I've included my two favorite pork tenderloin recipes here. The fried medallions can also work perfectly for pork chops.

Being on a strict food budget doesn't mean you have to live on Ramen noodles or do without things you love—it simply means you need to be more careful. Planning meals that utilize your leftovers, trying new things to avoid boredom, and cooking the same things in different ways are ways to begin as well as avoiding convenience foods and junk. Making a cake and frosting costs pennies compared to buying that same cake mix and (YUCKY!) frosting.

THIS IS AN EXAMPLE OF MEAL PLANNING FOR THIS WEEK:

SUNDAY: Breaded pork medallions w/mashed potatoes and asparagus (and leftover pork went into freezer.) This meal cost approximately four dollars total, AND I have two more meals worth of pork in the freezer! Less than a dollar.

MONDAY: Meatloaf w/ potato pancakes (made from leftover mashed potatoes.) Frozen broccoli in cheese sauce (got on sale for one dollar.) Another four dollars total for this meal, and I will have at least one lunch too. So two dollars each.

TUESDAY: Chicken Parmigiana and angel hair with bread (leftover in freezer.) Cost approximately three dollars to make two dinners worth. So

$1.50 each.

WEDNESDAY: BLT on homemade bread w/pickles and chips. Bacon was buy two, get three free. Lettuce at buy one, get one free. Tomatoes on sale. Meal total: $5.00 with leftovers for lunch.

THURSDAY: Homemade chicken breast tenders w/French fries. Lettuce and tomato salad (using leftovers from BLTs on Wednesday.) Chicken breasts were $1.99/lb. Half a breast used equals a half pound. French fries on sale two for four dollars—portion size equivalent to twenty-five cents. Meal cost approximately: $1.50 including oil for frying and breading materials.

FRIDAY: Pizza ziti with bread. Pizza ziti—1lb. hamburger $2.50, half pound of sweet sausage at 5 packages for $19.99—about $1.25. Half package pepperoni at buy two, get three free—about $1.00. One jar sauce $1.99. One can tomatoes $1.00. One can mushrooms $1.00. Peppers—had in freezer. One onion—had in fridge. Mozzarella cheese in freezer. Meatballs I had in freezer. Three quarter box ziti—10 for $10. Total cost: About $15.00-$18.00. I got six dinners from this. So $3.00 tops cost per meal. And this stuff was SO good!

So, if you notice, my meals usually cost between one and three dollars each and I don't eat crap. I don't live on box food or cheap junk. I eat well.

Pork medallions, chicken breasts, bacon, pasta loaded with meat and cheese. Every recipe I put in this book, I buy ingredients for, I cook, and I eat. I just plan what I will eat and when. I have no problem waiting for ribs to go on sale to buy them. I buy enough to last until next time they're on sale again. I pay attention to things like that. I know ribs are on sale about every six to seven weeks. So, when I buy my rack, I butcher them into two to three ribs per package, making enough packages for me to have ribs exactly once every week until they're on sale again. I pay between $1.29-$1.99/lb. when they're on sale. So let's say $2.00/lb. It's about $10.00 a rack. And I end up with a month and a half's worth of ribs. For $10. You can barely eat Ramen noodles for 6 weeks for $10, and I'm eating BBQ pork ribs. *Hell, yeah.*

So—are you ready to be a frugal eater now?

ROUNDING IT OUT

Molly

WHILE I DON'T focus a lot on fruits and vegetables in this book, they are important. I include them in one-dish recipes and as sides and snacks.

We typically have fruit with lunch or as snacks and a vegetable (or two) with dinner. Side salads are almost always on the table. I haven't included salad recipes because they are created to personal tastes and, by nature, are inexpensive. I will say it's wise to consider getting creative, especially if you are used to eating prepared salads or buying out. Using leftover ham, pork, chicken or turkey, and even leftover vegetables can make unique and frugal salads. Make your own dressings.

For vegetables, I've narrowed our family's list down to the ones we will all eat. It makes me feel good to buy all variety of vegetables, but if they don't eat it, I'll feel worse having to throw it away.

Occasionally, I will buy Brussel sprouts (which only my husband will eat.) He and I love peas, but the kids don't. To avoid waste, I won't buy as much of what isn't eaten by all. I focus on broccoli, corn, carrots, and green beans, in that order. Two greens, a yellow, and an orange. Over the course of the month, everyone gets what they need, and everyone likes what they get.

When I can, I buy fresh. Otherwise, like everything else, I try to buy in bulk. Three- and five-pound bags of frozen works well. Canned is the last option, and while I don't believe this is as nutritious, it's better than nothing. I prefer to home can when possible, but not everyone is able to do that. (For the sake of ultimate frugality, please do look into it. It's really not that hard.)

Buying by the case, especially when there is a sale, can help stack a few dozen cans of each vegetable (save broccoli) tucked away.

Remember, if you've got it, you can skip buying it for a month or two, and that really comes in handy if your budget takes an even tighter squeeze.

The same goes for fruit, though there are many more fruits that are eaten by everyone in this house.

I try to buy what's in season so it narrows down the fruit list in the winter, but that's when I rely on canned peaches, pears, and apples. (And lately, dehydrated fruits.)

Late spring through early fall, apples, bananas, strawberries, raspberries, and blueberries are always in this house. Not in mass quantities as I buy them weekly. Again, my boys will eat fruit all day, and if I buy more than a week's worth, it will go too quickly. If your budget constrains you to buy less variety, and your family likes it, go with bananas, apples, and oranges. A yellow, red, and orange and you're covered.

Sometimes, I will buy a five-pound bag of blueberries at Costco for less than ten dollars. I am sure to can this up in pints (or divide into baggies with a clear rule of one per day per person for snacking,) or else I'll wake up and find half the bag gone and blue-stained lips on boys both saying, "It wasn't me."

Same with the more expensive raspberries. Creating baggies with names or limits (or off limits) is a good way to get the more expensive fruits to last. (And always set aside what you'll need for recipes first if your kids are fruit monsters like mine!)

That's about all I have to say on fruits and veggies. Get as much as you can because it's healthy and will offset some of the carbs in the tastier dishes in this book.

VEGETABLES

Daisy

I AM NOT huge on veggies either, but I will eat more of them if they are mixed with other things, like stir-fry or soup. Any veggie made into a fritter becomes my new best friend. Who can resist crispy fried anything?

Fruit—I just don't eat it unless it's dessert.... Pie? Yes, please! I prefer cooked fruit over raw.

MEAT

Molly

For most of the country, the modern idea of "a steak on every plate" is being replaced with the old adage of "a chicken in every pot."

I TYPICALLY SPEND a hundred dollars or less a month on meat for a family of four. That might seem like a little or a lot depending on your family and position. I'm rather proud of it, though. I'm not anti-meat, either. I love it. I just don't like spending a lot of money. Here's how a typical month breaks down for us. (Current prices for my location as of this writing.)

- One ham $18
- Ten pounds very lean hamburger $40
- One whole chicken $5
- Three pounds bacon ends and pieces $5
- Ten pounds chicken quarters $8
- Two pounds sausage $5
- Five pounds boneless pork fillets $6
- Total: $87

Depending on the menu and price fluctuations, this list occasionally pushes the hundred-dollar mark, but that's still pretty darn good.

Cost could be driven down even more by replacing some of the hamburger with chicken, but this is a good balance for us, and it tends to prevent food weariness.

HERE'S HOW I break that down to make an entire month of meals.

We have ham with all the sides (sort of a mini thanksgiving) once a month. Of course, four of us barely put a dent into a whole ham, so I divide up the rest into baggies. It makes between eight and ten more 'meals.' I use that with breakfast, for sandwiches (spiral sliced ham is good for this), soups, stews, casseroles, and occasionally, just reheating ham slices with mashed potatoes and gravy. (And a veggie. Don't forget the veggie.)

The hamburger, I divide up into three-quarter pound chubs and wrap in saran wrap. I get thirteen dinners out of one ten-pound roll of meat, and no one has noticed the difference. I will use two of them if I make meatloaf or hamburger patties, but for other meals like casseroles, tacos, and nachos, I use the three-quarter pound chubs, and it works fine.

The ten pounds of chicken quarters, I boil in a very large stockpot for several hours. When it's all cooked, I let it cool and debone everything (saving out a few for that night's dinner because I'm beat.) I end up with about eight sandwich bags of chicken meat. We use this for chopped chicken sandwiches, casseroles, soups, stews, salads, and whatever else I need to throw in a few cups of chopped chicken.

Bacon ends and pieces, I don't use for bacon. I make bacon bits. (Though you could pick out several of the more regular slices and use those for a breakfast meat.) I grind it all in my hand crank grinder—really cheap, not that hard to find, and you can mark a workout off your daily to-do list. Then I fry it all in my deep cast iron pan on medium heat so it doesn't burn. When the bacon crumbles look good, are dark red, and all the fat has separated away, I drain off the 'bacon bits' from the fat using cheesecloth into pint jars. I get about a pint and a half of real bacon bits and another pint and a half of bacon fat to use in cooking. (Not bad for five bucks.) Both the bacon and the fat give amazing flavor to anything you use it in. I almost always add a tablespoon of bacon bits to eggs in the morning. All the flavor, fraction of the fat. Actually, considering I save butter by using a teaspoon of bacon fat to make those eggs, it all evens out in the end. It just tastes really good. Again, soups, stews, casseroles, sandwiches, salads—throw in some of these wherever you want a bacon punch to your recipe.

The sausage, in this house, is only used for two things. Biscuits and gravy and thin patties for sausage, egg, and cheese biscuits. I normally make both at the same time on a Sunday morning. I'll use a third of a pound of the sausage for gravy and the rest in patties. One-ounce patties will make six to eight patties. Not much by itself but plenty for a breakfast biscuit.

The boneless pork fillets/chops most often end up in the Crock-Pot for two separate dinners. Five pounds usually end up being eight chops. I'll do one Italian and one BBQ. Or slow cook barbecue chops all night and bag up for pulled lunch meat for the week.

MORE TIPS AND TRICKS:

BUY LOWER FAT hamburger. I know it's more expensive, but you end up with more actual meat when you buy the lowest fat you can. It drives me nuts to pay for unusable grease in a pan. Also, if you try to divide high-fat meat into three-quarter pound chubs, you won't end up with nearly as much when it's cooked.

Buy chicken quarters and separate to make your own chicken thighs and legs. I recently saw chicken thighs on sale for $1.20/lb. Legs were $.99/lb. Chicken quarters were $.87/lb. in bulk ten pound frozen bags. It's the same meat!! It just requires the added step of separating it yourself, which isn't that hard to do.

Tuna and other fish. I really like tuna but eat very little of it. As if the rising mercury levels weren't enough, there was just something about the Fukushima fallout that changed my view on tuna and seafood. My husband still asks for a couple cans of tuna a month for sandwich variety, but I no longer make meals with it. If you are still comfortable using it, tuna and other fish can make great frugal meals, as well.

Outside of a turkey and corned beef for Thanksgiving and St. Patrick's Day (my monthly ham is used on Christmas), those are the meats I use throughout the year.

DAIRY

Molly

I WILL OUTLINE what I use and how I buy it, and from there, you can find out what works for you and your family. I have a pretty standard, rotating list of what I buy that works really well. I normally buy dairy every two weeks. My list is so repetitive even my husband could shop for me now. Ours has become very routine. Yours will vary depending on your family's needs. But you will notice that you'll fall into a pattern.

MONTHLY DAIRY INCLUDES:

- Eight gallons of milk $14 (very cheap right now)
- Four pounds shredded cheddar cheese $12
- Two pounds shredded Mozzarella cheese $6
- Three pounds cream cheese $6 (Costco)
- Two pounds cottage cheese $5 (Costco)
- Eight pounds butter $16 (Costco)
- Ten dozen medium eggs $8 (also extremely cheap right now)
- Two pounds sour cream $4
- One can powdered milk $14

You can find ten-pound cans of powdered milk in the bulk or preparedness section of almost any store now. It is cheaper to buy it this way than to buy the boxes of carnation milk on the baking aisle. Also, I buy one a month whether

I'm out or not. This way I've been able to keep a few on hand all the time. You know, in case the zombies come. (wink)

Total for dairy: $85

And now, finally, recipes!

BREADS

Molly

BREAD IS THE foundation of a simple diet. And not store bought bread, either. Thick, filling slices of home baked bread.

I make our bread almost all of the time. I need to bake two loaves or one super loaf every other day for a family of four. Wilton makes a fantastic long pan. When I was getting started, I used small dollar store bread tins.

I also make our hamburger, hot dog buns and pizza dough as well as biscuits.

BREAD

6 cups flour
3 Tbsp. sugar
1 Tbsp. salt
2 Tbsp. shortening
2 pkgs. yeast
(One package of yeast is 2 1/4 tsp. if you buy in bulk as I do)
2 1/4 cups warm water

I mix 4 cups of flour with the sugar, salt, yeast, shortening, and water. Mix by hand or with a dough hook in a mixer until well blended. Add the remaining flour one cup at a time and knead until it forms dough you can handle. Knead for fifteen minutes by hand or seven minutes in the mixer. Cover and let rise an hour.

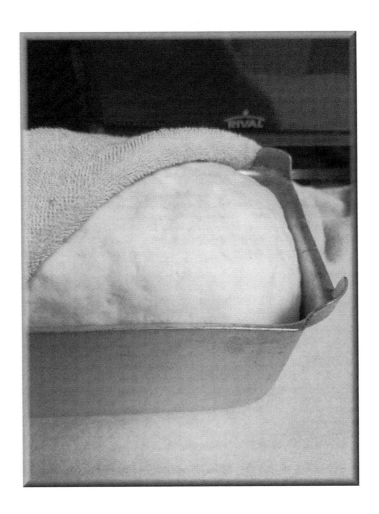

Remove dough and knead for a few minutes on the counter before forming loaves and placing in an oiled pan. This will make two small loaves or one long loaf. Cover for about an hour. (I find this depends on the weather. Hot days, it will raise the dough in forty minutes, cold days could be over an hour.) I gauge it by the pan. When it's raised an inch over the edge of the pan, I put it in the oven.

Bake at 425 (short pan) or 375 (long pan) for 25-30 minutes. The top should be golden brown and sound hollow when tapped. I like to rub the tops with butter right out of the oven. It makes for a softer top crust.

That's all there is to it.

I was so nervous when I started making bread. I followed every step of the directions to a T, down to the minute, and obsessed if I was doing it right. Some recipes call for dissolving yeast in warm water for five minutes. Personally, I don't do that. Some say knead in mixer for fifteen minutes. I set the mixer to go and do some laundry or cook something else. My knead times always vary. I figured out pretty quick that bread was super easy to make and as long as you don't kill the yeast by using too hot water, you'll always end up with something edible. Now, I don't set a timer for rising, kneading, or baking. I can see by the size that it's raised enough I know by the feel that it's kneaded enough, and I can smell when it's done. The hollow tap is just confirmation. The more you make your own bread, the easier it will seem.

Here are some of the things I use my bread for beyond sandwiches...just to name a few:

- French toast
- garlic bread
- croutons
- grilled cheese
- homemade hot pockets (in an electric sandwich maker)
- toasted slices under chipped beef and gravy
- cinnamon toast
- cheese toast
- bread pudding

HOT DOG/HAMBURGER BUNS

2 Tbsp. yeast
1 cup + 2 Tbsp. warm water
1/3 cup oil
1/4 cup sugar
1 tsp. salt
3 - 3 1/2 cups flour

Mix 3 cups of flour with the yeast, water, oil, sugar, and salt. Mix well and knead as it forms dough. Add the remaining 1/2 cup of flour a little at a time until you have dough you can handle easily.

No rising needed if you don't have time. Just shape into hot dog or hamburger buns. Place on a cookie sheet and let rest on the top of the stove while it's preheating to 425. Bake for 8-12 minutes. Makes about 1 dozen. (For the life of me, I can't get more than ten buns out of this.)

I brush mine with butter when they come out of the oven and let cool before I cut. For the hot dog buns, cut long ways, a little past half way down with a bread knife.

These are very, very filling. Even my teenager struggles to eat two when there is a side like fries or potato salad. The rest of us only manage one. They hold up very well to toppings like chili and melted cheese.

Leftover buns can be used for mini garlic breads, mini subs, and French dips.

BASIC PIZZA DOUGH

3 cups flour
1 pkg yeast (2 1/4 tsp.)

2 Tbsp. oil

1 tsp. salt

1 Tbsp. sugar

1 cup warm water

Combine flour, salt, sugar, and yeast. Add water and oil. Mix until blended then knead for five minutes. Use immediately or let rise until doubled in size, punch down, and then roll out as pizza crust. No rise will result in a thin crust. Rising will result in a thicker one. Place on a well-oiled pan. Top with pizza sauce. I make my own, but I have used canned spaghetti sauce in a pinch. It works fine. Add cheese and whatever meats or veggies you like. Bake at 375 for about 20 minutes. Makes two medium pizzas or one large sheet pizza.

Yum! Fresh out of the oven and ready to eat.

BULK BISCUIT MIX

10 cups flour

1/2 cup baking powder

2 tsp. salt

2 cups shortening (or lard)

In a large bowl (I use a Kitchen Aid with the whisk attachment), mix flour, baking powder, and salt. But it can easily be done by hand. Cut in shortening and mix until it is completely incorporated and slightly crumbly. It should look like coarse flour.

TO MAKE A BATCH OF BISCUITS USE:

2 1/2 cups mix

1 egg

1/2 cup milk (might need to add more depending on altitude.)

This recipe worked fine at sea level. Now that I'm in the mountains, I find I need to add a Tbsp. or more milk. Play with it until it looks like smooth dough that you can handle.

Roll out and cut the biscuits. I go about an inch thick and use one of my glasses that make the perfect size. Bake at 425 for 15 minutes.

BULK PANCAKE MIX

12 cups flour

4 cups instant nonfat milk

1 cup baking powder

1 cup sugar

1 Tbsp. salt

Mix well and store in an airtight container.

To use:

2 cups mix

1 egg

3 Tbsp. oil

1 cup of water (more or less for consistency)

Stir until smooth and cook as normal in a little oil. This can convert to a waffle recipe easily by adding a little less water to make a thicker batter. Pour into a waffle iron and bake normally.

CAN'T HAVE PANCAKES or waffles without syrup! Here's the most basic recipe that I use.

PANCAKE SYRUP

Use Mapleine for that classic maple flavor at a fraction of the price.
1 cup sugar
1 cup brown sugar
3/4 cup water
2 tsp. Mapleine

Mix all over medium heat stirring constantly. Slowly bring to a boil and boil for three minutes. Makes about a pint. It says this recipe can be canned, so if you wanted to multiply the ingredients by ten and can in pint jars, you'd have it on the shelf creating your own convenient staple.

PUMPKIN BREAD

Great for quick breakfasts, snacks, or dessert.
Makes two loaves

3 cups sugar
1 cup oil
4 eggs
1 tsp. nutmeg
1 tsp. cinnamon
1 ½ tsp. salt
2 cups pumpkin
⅔ cup water
1 tsp. baking soda
½ tsp. baking powder
3 cups flour

Combine sugar, oil, eggs, spices, and salt. Blend well. Add remaining ingredients and mix well until all lumps are gone. Pour into two oiled loaf pans. Bake at 350 for 1 hour.

BANANA BREAD

Great for quick breakfasts, snacks, or dessert.

½ cup butter
1 cup sugar
2 eggs

1 tsp. vanilla
1 ½ cups flour
1 tsp. baking soda
½ tsp. salt
½ cup sour cream
2 medium bananas

Mix butter and sugar. Add eggs and vanilla. Mix well. Add the rest of the ingredients and beat well. Pour into one oiled loaf pan. Bake at 450 for 45-55 minutes.

DAISY'S BREADS

WHEN I WAS newly single, I ate a lot of bread. Sandwiches were a regular part of my diet. I had them for dinner several times a week rather than cooking for myself. After being a family of six, then a couple, it was hard to adjust to being a single person and only caring for myself. After a few months, I gave up the sandwiches and began cooking real meals for myself. Since then, it's been a constant struggle to use bread before it turns blue and fuzzy. I love hard-crusted bread like French bread or a good chewy Italian loaf or give me real pumpernickel, and I'm in heaven. When I found myself so disgusted with the offerings in the stores, I started making my own. I gave away my bread machine in favor of the therapeutic benefits of making my own bread.

There's something that brings me closer to the ones that came before me when I'm kneading bread. The rawness of this simple work calms my mind and takes me to a place I know I've never been, yet strangely, I feel, I still should be.

My hands move on their own in a rhythm. The dough whispers to them as my mind wanders across a long ago prairie searching for the place where the wheat grows tall and golden. I see men with strong backs gathering these yellow bundles, then grandmothers sewing curtains from the flour sacks. As my bread bakes, and I smell its yeasty wonder, I hear children running and clambering, hardly able to wait for it to leave the oven and cool... mouths watering, yelling over who will have the first piece. I bake bread not only for the amazing bread it gives me but also for the connection that this simple thing gives me to my ancestors and the history of my world. *Oh.... Okay, I'm back now... What a journey I was on there for a moment!*

Baking bread also connects me more fully to my food. It helps me to be more cognizant of what I'm eating and of food waste. Think about it. If you put two hours of your time and work into baking your bread, you're going to be much more careful about wasting it... because that's two more hours of your time and work needed when it's gone. If you buy your bread for three dollars, are you really going to be as diligent about not wasting it?

So, having said all that, here are a couple of recipes for bread that I love. My very favorite is French bread. It's super easy, soft centered with that crisp, chewy crust, and so perfect for dipping into soups, stews or for sandwiches too. The other—artisan bread—has gotten rave reviews from a number of my friends.

FAST AND EASY FRENCH BREAD

¼-cup warm (not hot) water (this water the yeast will be dissolved in)
2 ½ tsp. active dry yeast
1 tsp. sugar
3 ½–4 cups flour
1 Tbsp. sugar

1 tsp. salt

1 cup +1 Tbsp. warm water (this goes in the flour)

1 egg white and 1 Tbsp. water (to brush on top of bread before baking)

Combine first 3 ingredients in a large bowl. Allow to stand until yeast is bubbly. Then add in the second set of ingredients—flour last and 1 cup at a time, mixing well.

Knead for 5 minutes. Let rise in warm place for 15-20 minutes.

Place on floured surface. Flatten with rolling pin to 1 inch. Roll up jellyroll style and turn ends under. Place seam side down on OILED cookie sheet and cut 3 diagonal cuts ½ inch deep in top.

Combine egg white and water. Brush on top of bread.

Preheat oven to 300F. Boil a pan of water and pour into shallow oven safe dish. TURN OVEN OFF and place dish on lower rack in oven. Place bread in oven, and let rise until doubled. Take out water, but leave in the bread as you preheat oven to 425. Bake for 10 minutes. Turn oven back down to 375 and bake for 8 more minutes or until golden brown.

NO KNEAD, ARTISAN BREAD

THE BEST THING about this bread is that it's very customizable. I have made it and added garlic powder, minced dried onion, parmesan cheese, parsley, chopped sunflower seeds and sea salt—and it was like an "everything" bagel. Yum! I have also made the same recipe and added whole oats, walnuts, raisins, cinnamon, nutmeg, and a few spoonfuls of applesauce. Whatever you like, sweet or savory. Mix up about 1 ½ – 1 ¾ cups of it.

After the dough is ready, create a space in the center of the dough ball for approximately one cup of your additions. Put them in and twist the dough closed around them. Don't pull too tight, but be sure whatever you're adding is tucked inside. Top your bread with the rest.

Now here is the SECOND best thing about this bread:

It bakes in your Crock-Pot.

This is going to be your new favorite bread, I can tell. Makes two round/oval loaves.

1 ½ cup lukewarm water
½ Tbsp. active dry yeast
¾ Tbsp. salt
3 ¼ cup flour

You may want to play with the salt yourself, adding more or less to suit your taste. When adding a filling to this bread, especially a sweet one, more salt may be desired in order to have the sweet/salty effect. When adding a savory filling, you may want to use less salt.

Put water in bowl. Add yeast and salt. Add flour all at once and mix until flour is incorporated. It will make a rough, wet dough. Cover loosely. Allow to sit at room temperature two hours to rise. Do not punch down. Let it settle itself.

At this point, you can refrigerate it or use it. It will keep up to two weeks in the fridge and makes two loaves. If you refrigerate it, let rest for 40 minutes before baking.

Form into two balls. Place one on parchment paper and lower into Crock-Pot turned on high. Refrigerate the other unless you have two Crock-Pots. After 45 minutes, check to make sure it's not over browning. Cook in Crock-Pot for one hour. Bread will be baked but not browned on top or sides. The bottom should be crispy, but the top will be quite soft.

Remove from Crock-Pot and from parchment paper and place under oven broiler for 5 minutes or until top is desired brownness. Let cool before slicing.

I HAVE GOTTEN rave reviews for this next bread, but I can't tell you myself how it is because I don't like cinnamon bread, but I do enjoy making it. It makes a fantastic gift. Use Molly's recipe for your dough, and in no time, you will have a beautiful loaf baked up and ready to eat—or to give to someone special.

CINNAMON SWIRL RAISIN BREAD

Dough for 1 loaf of bread plus the following:
1 ½ Tbsp. water
¼ cup sugar
1 Tbsp. cinnamon
2 Tbsp. melted butter
½ cup raisins

On lightly floured surface, roll out bread dough with rolling pin. Roll into 10" x 12" rectangle. Paint dough with water then sprinkle sugar and cinnamon over dough and top with raisins.

Roll up tightly, beginning on the long side. Seal all seams and ends.

Cut into two pieces with sharp knife.

Twist the two pieces together to form a swirled loaf. Place in GREASED 8x4 loaf pan and brush with butter.

Let rise in warm place until doubled in size then bake at 350F for 30 minutes. Remove from pan to cool.

WHERE I LIVE, there are two things people like to eat from a pizza place, besides pizza—hot wings and garlic knots. If you aren't familiar with garlic knots, you're missing out. They're delicious, knotted pillows of pizza dough, baked perfectly then painted with melted butter, garlic and parmesan cheese while they're still hot from the oven. Try them. They are a great snack or dipper for spaghetti and meatballs, they pair nicely with green salads, and they reheat well in the oven too.

GARLIC KNOTS

Dough:
1 ½ cups warm water
2 ¼ tsp. active dry yeast
2 Tbsp. oil
3 ½ -4 ½ cups flour
1 tsp. salt
1 Tbsp. sugar

Butter for topping:
2 Tbsp. butter
2 cloves minced garlic
¼ tsp. garlic powder
4 Tbsp. Parmesan cheese

Combine water, sugar, and yeast in a large bowl and stir. Let sit for 10 minutes or until it is foamy. Add in the oil and mix. Stir in flour, some at a time, and add the salt. The dough will be sticky but should not be too wet. If it is too wet, add more flour 1 Tbsp. at a time until it becomes manageable. You should be able to form a ball with it.

Turn dough out onto lightly floured surface and knead for five minutes, then place dough in large greased bowl, turn the dough so that all sides are coated with oil and cover the bowl with oiled plastic wrap. Let rise until doubled in size, about an hour.

Preheat oven to 400F

Remove the dough from the bowl and place on lightly floured surface once more. Cut into 16 equal pieces. Roll each piece like you're making a snake out of clay. Each piece needs to be a dough rope of 9-10 inches in length and about ½ inch thick.

Shape into a knot by folding one end over the other—like an awareness ribbon, and twist the dough back at the place where the two sides overlap and tuck under.

OR—the easy way—tie the dough into a knot and leave the ends out.

Place knots on a cookie sheet lined with parchment paper and bake for 10-12 minutes or until golden brown.

Make the garlic butter topping by melting butter in a saucepan on the stove. When the butter is melted, stir in garlic and garlic powder. Brush this over the baked knots and sprinkle with parmesan cheese. Enjoy warm or at room temperature.

Reheat leftovers in a 400-degree oven on cookie sheet for 6-8 minutes.

Can be frozen. Freeze after baking and top with garlic butter after reheating.

BREAKFAST

Breakfast with Molly

BREAKFASTS ARE USUALLY based on the foundation of a simple diet—homemade bread. Options around here include:

- Eggs and toast (sausage patties/bacon if on sale)
- French toast
- Pancakes
- Waffles
- Oatmeal with milk/brown sugar or fruit
- Popovers
- Muffins
- Biscuits and gravy
- Breakfast biscuits
- Breakfast burritos
- Cinnamon rolls

You'll find the recipes for most of these below. I won't outline eggs or French toast. I'm sure you've already got that covered.

POPOVERS

Perfect for chilly mornings with butter and jam.

2 eggs
1 cup milk
1 cup flour

Mix all ingredients well. Pour into oiled or papered muffin cups three-quarters full. Place in a cold oven, heat to 450 and bake for 30 minutes.

Top with butter, jam, apple butter, etc.

BULK INSTANT OATMEAL

This recipe calls for dehydrated or freeze-dried fruit. You can omit this completely or substitute with fresh fruit if you'd like.

12 cups instant oatmeal
1 cup brown sugar
2 Tbsp. cinnamon
4 cups dehydrated/freeze dried fruit
1 cup instant milk powder

Mix well and store in an airtight container.

To use, add ½ cup boiling water to ¾ cup of mix in a bowl. Cover and let sit for three minutes. If you are using whole or steel cut oats, add another tablespoon of water and consider cooking on the stove at medium-low heat for about 8 minutes.

Variations include using pumpkin pie spice or nutmeg with or instead of cinnamon, raisins, peanut butter, or chocolate chips.

I make one batch of this as stated above with freeze-dried strawberries. I make another batch without fruit so we can customize each bowl with fresh fruit, applesauce, butter and milk or a sprinkle of chocolate.

I make a half batch of "autumn oatmeal" using pumpkin pie spice and dehydrated or freeze-dried apples.

This is always enough to last through the winter and into spring.

MORNING MUFFINS

I CALL THEM morning but really, they are great for snacks or to pack with lunches, too.

The recipe calls for a cake mix so be sure to buy those on sale to keep costs down. Normally, I love to make everything from scratch, but I've yet to find a recipe that creates such dense, moist muffins as this does. (I'm still on the hunt!) I'll list out the recipe and then the possible variations below.

1 yellow cake mix
1 tsp. baking powder
2 Tbsp. flour
⅓ cup oil
3 eggs.
⅔ cup milk
1-2 cups blueberries

Preheat oven to 375. Mix all ingredients but the milk in a mixing bowl. Add most of the ⅔ cup of milk and stir well. You may or may not use all of the milk. The batter needs to be the consistency of brownie batter; it should mostly cling to the spoon when turned upside down. When you achieve that, stop adding milk. Add blueberries and fill a greased muffin tin or muffin papers three-fourths of the way full. Bake for 15-20 minutes.

Variations include using any fruit you'd like with a white or yellow cake mix. You can also use chocolate (or any flavor) chips. Chocolate cake mix with peanut butter chips is tasty for a snack muffin, as is raspberries added to a white cake mix for a breakfast muffin.

CINNAMON ROLLS

THIS RECIPE USES the hot dog/hamburger bun recipe. I discovered it by mistake. I was harried, cooking dinner, prepping breakfast for the next day and jotting down recipe ideas for this book all at the same time. I flipped open my personal cookbook and began throwing dough together. Only after, did I notice it was the hot dog bun recipe! I thought, "Well, I'm not throwing it out so let's see what happens." What happened was my husband requesting I never make cinnamon rolls any other way again. So here's the hot dog bun recipe again so you don't have to flip back.

2 Tbsp. yeast
1 cup + 2 Tbsp. warm water
1/3 cup oil
1/4 cup sugar
1 tsp. salt
3 - 3 1/2 cups flour

Mix 3 cups of flour with the yeast, water, oil, sugar, and salt. Mix well and knead as it forms dough. Add the remaining 1/2 cup of flour a little at a time until you have dough you can handle easily. Cover and let rise for half hour to an hour. Roll out into a large rectangle. The dough should be no more than a half-inch thick. Spread with softened butter (½ to ¾ cup) and then sprinkle generously with a mixture of cinnamon and sugar. I always keep a jar of cinnamon sugar in the cupboard. I use 1 cup of sugar with 2 Tbsp. cinnamon. After you've sprinkled on the cinnamon sugar mixture, begin rolling up the dough along the long end. When it's rolled, pinch the dough along the final seam so it won't unroll while baking. I use a serrated knife or waxed dental floss to cut the rolls about 1 ½ inches thick. This recipe always makes twelve rolls for me. Put in a casserole pan or cookie sheet with sides. Let the cinnamon rolls rise again (15 minutes, give or take) as the oven is preheating to 350. Bake for about 25 minutes, until the tops are golden brown.

Make a simple glaze by mixing ½ cup butter with three cups confectioners' sugar and ½ tsp. vanilla. Add milk one tsp. at a time until the desired consistency is met, from a thick, spreadable frosting to a thin glaze to drizzle. These will store well for a few days under plastic wrap.

BREAKFAST BISCUITS

BREAKFAST BISCUITS ARE a huge hit in this house and freeze well. I usually make a double batch of biscuits on the morning that I'm making biscuits and gravy. I'll fry one egg and one thin sausage patty for each biscuit. If I don't have sausage, I'll sprinkle homemade bacon bits on each egg and let it cook in, or use some of the ham I've portioned off earlier in the month. I will use either slice cheese or, more often, sprinkle shredded cheddar on a halved biscuit and add the egg and sausage. Put the top on and let cool. Wrap individually in plastic wrap and store in the freezer. These will heat in the microwave for two minutes from frozen, forty-five seconds if thawed.

BREAKFAST BURRITOS

ANOTHER GOOD BULK breakfast that freezes well. I buy up tortillas when they are on sale. Scramble a dozen eggs, then add hash brown or diced potatoes (cooked), crumbled cooked bacon, chopped ham, or sausage. If you like peppers, mushrooms, and onions, add those, too. Mix everything together and then spoon into tortillas and roll. After they've cooled completely, wrap in saran wrap and freeze. Heat for two minutes if frozen, forty-five seconds if thawed.

T AND T'S WAFFLED FRENCH TOAST

THIS RECIPE WILL make you happy all the way down to your toes. I made the stuffed French toast part of it for two kids that have been like my own. They loved all of my breakfasts. Today, I put the stuffed French toast in the waffle iron...the kids weren't here—they're not even kids anymore, but I know they would have approved. So, these delights are named after them. I love you, Ted and Tiff.

Heat up your waffle iron. Spray it with vegetable oil spray.

4 eggs
Vegetable Oil Spray
4 slices of bread with crusts removed
2 Tbsp. cream cheese, softened
½ tsp. cinnamon
1 Tbsp. Blueberry Preserves
2 Tbsp. water
Powdered sugar

Beat the eggs with the water and add cinnamon. Mix cream cheese with blueberry preserves and set aside. Dip all slices of bread in egg mixture. When waffle iron is hot, put two dipped slices of bread in waffle iron. Close and cook for one min. Open, and top each piece of bread with half of the cream cheese mixture, and then the other pieces of egg-dipped bread. Close waffle maker again and cook until top is golden brown. Note: Some of the cream cheese and blueberry mixture may leak out. Don't worry. There will be plenty left. When done, sprinkle with powdered sugar or top with whipped topping or maple syrup. Whatever you like.

And enjoy!

THESE CAN TAKE you from breakfast all the way to dinner, but you'll want to stop and have one or two for lunch. They're savory and go great with sausage and eggs...but a little sweet maple syrup on them makes them pure heaven. Not just for breakfast, they're terrific reheated as leftovers.

BACON CORN CAKES
Makes 6

6 slices of bacon, cut into ½ pieces
1 egg, beaten
⅓ cup chopped onion
1 Tbsp. veg oil
1 cup flour
1 tsp. baking powder
8 oz. can whole kernel corn, drained
½ cup shredded Monterey Jack
½ tsp. salt warm maple syrup
⅛ tsp. cayenne pepper
⅔ cup milk

Cook bacon and onion over med-high heat until bacon is browned, 7-9 minutes. In a med. bowl, combine flour, baking powder, salt, and cayenne pepper. Stir in milk, egg, oil just until moistened. Stir in bacon and onion and remaining ingredients except maple syrup. Heat pan or griddle to 350 degrees. Pour ⅓ cup batter onto griddle for each corn cake. Cook until sides are golden brown 3-4 minutes each. Serve warm with warm maple syrup.

PEANUT BUTTER AND JELLY PANCAKES

ANOTHER OF MY T and T favs… Kids love these, and I have to say, I find them pretty yummy myself! With Molly's bulk pancake mix, super easy too!

Make plain pancake batter. Here's how with Molly's bulk pancake mix:

2 cups mix
1 egg
3 Tbsp. oil
1 cup of water

Then, melt ¾ cup peanut butter in the microwave and stir into batter. Cook pancakes as usual...when pancakes are nearly done, put ½–¾ cup blueberry or strawberry preserves in the microwave—whatever you like—with 2 Tbsp. water and warm until liquefied. Pour over pancakes and enjoy.

SPICED DONUT PUFFS

NOW THIS IS my kind of breakfast. These donuts are baked in a muffin tin, making them a healthier version of the fried variety. All the flavor, none of the fat. You'll never miss it...and no remorse, what's better than frugal guilt-free donuts? Not ONE thing.

2 Tbsp. shortening
½ cup sugar
1 egg
2 cup flour
½ tsp. salt
1 Tbsp. baking powder
½ tsp. nutmeg
½ cup milk
¼ cup confectioners' sugar
½ tsp. cinnamon
¼ cup melted butter

Preheat oven to 400 degrees.

Cream shortening, sugar, and egg until fluffy. Mix flour, salt, baking powder, and nutmeg well. And add alternately with milk to shortening mixture. Mix this well. It will be stiff dough.

Drop from Tbsp. into well-greased muffin pan cups.

Bake at 400 for 20 minutes.

Combine confectioners' sugar and cinnamon in paper bag, dip tops of donuts in melted butter, quickly, and shake 2-3 at a time in paper bag.

Serve hot.

Makes 1 dozen.

FRENCH TOAST SAUSAGE ROLLS

THESE LOVELIES CAN be a wonderful breakfast or a great breakfast-for-dinner. Make them with Molly's hot dog roll recipe, pair them with my waffle potatoes, and you have a stick-to-your-ribs frugal meal that'll make your wallet and your tummy happy.

12 pork sausage links
6 eggs
⅓ cup milk
Salt and pepper to taste
6 hot dog buns

Cook sausages until well done, then set aside.

Beat together the eggs milk and S+P, dip hot dog buns in egg mixture, and cook on both sides in hot oiled pan until browned...like French toast.

Place 2 sausages in each bun and serve with syrup.

Makes 6 servings

LUNCH

Daisy

WE DON'T HAVE any specific recipes for this section because the absolute go-to for lunches is to first use up leftovers from the night before. Soup and sandwich or soup and salad are next in line, combined with fruit or a snack treat. Some of the dinner dishes we'll share in the next section can be made in smaller batches and used for lunch as well.

I agree with Molly 100% on that, and I think leftovers from the night before can make some of the best lunches and, I might add, breakfasts too…. but those are other recipes.

Today for lunch, I created this dish from my leftover chicken thighs and a few things I had on hand. It's amazing what you can put together from a few ingredients if you think about it for a minute.

I *always* have dried bread on hand. Since I don't eat a lot of bread, it happens. I turn it into breadcrumbs and stuffing. Before its breadcrumbs, it's a bag of dried bread in my fridge. This is convenient so that whenever I want to make an impromptu stuffing, I have a supply of bread for it. Today was such a day.

I had homemade chicken stock and chopped celery in my freezer, and leftover chicken thighs from last night...leftovers were about to become lunch.

DINNERS

WAFFLED CHICKEN AND STUFFING

Spray oil
½ lg. onion
2 Tbsp. butter
¼ cup chopped celery
Meat from 2 cooked chicken thighs, chopped
4-5 slices very dry bread
1 egg
1 Tbsp. poultry seasoning
1 Tbsp. parsley
1 ½ cups chicken stock—homemade or canned
½ tsp. my Simple Sausage Seasoning (included in this book)

Turn on waffle iron to heat.

Brown chopped onion and celery in butter on med. to high heat so they are deeply browned, then deglaze the pan with ½ cup chicken stock and turn heat down to slow simmer the veggies until the onions are done and not crunchy.

In a bowl, mix all of your seasonings, chicken, bread, 1 egg and the remainder of the chicken stock. Mix well.

Coat all grids of the waffle iron with spray oil. Using tongs, fill the waffle molds with the stuffing and chicken mix. Mine took about three heaping tablespoons. Close tightly. The mixture will spread out and fill.

Cook until outside of waffle stuffing is golden brown. Don't overcook.

Serve with either warm gravy or warm cranberry sauce glaze. That recipe follows.

CRANBERRY SAUCE GLAZE

1 can jellied cranberry sauce
½ cup water
½ cup orange juice
½ cup brown sugar

Put all ingredients into a pan and bring to a boil. Turn down then stir and simmer until sugar is dissolved and sauce begins to reduce and thicken. Refrigerate. An excellent glaze for baking on ham, chicken, pork chops, loins, and turkey.

QUICK AND EASY

I USED TO LOVE Jiffy mix and Bisquick. It's the best stuff. Very overpriced, it's one of the first things I struck from my grocery list when I became single. Jiffy and Bisquick did the measuring and the work for me. I didn't have to add baking soda or baking powder to my flour, nothing—just wet ingredients...and maybe sugar if I was making a dessert dish. I used it for pancakes, coffee cake, cookies, dumplings, and biscuits, of course.

I'd been going through my old cookbooks yesterday and came across some of my old Jiffy Mix recipes that I had handwritten and stuffed in the back of one of them. Suddenly, I had a lightbulb moment! Could it really be true?!

The amazing Molly has given us real cooking Nirvana with her *BULK BISCUIT MIX.*

Once again, my Jiffy recipes can come out of the back of my cookbook and be used. Oh yay! I have some great ones too!

IN A JIFFY CHICKEN POT PIE

Preheat oven to 450
1 can of cream of chicken soup
¼ cup milk
1 cup diced cooked chicken
1 1/2 cup cooked or 1 can drained mixed vegetables of your choice—I use peas and carrots.

TOPPING:

1 cup BULK BISCUIT MIX
½ cup milk
Salt and pepper to taste

Combine first four ingredients and pour into a small baking pan. Mix topping ingredients and spoon over the mixture in pan. Bake at 450 for 25 minutes or until topping is nicely browned. Serve hot.

IN A JIFFY COFFEE CAKE

THIS COFFEECAKE IS a perfect copy of the little ones that came two in a package when I was a kid. It's a great breakfast or after school snack or bedtime treat… or anytime grab.

2 cups BULK BISCUIT MIX
2 Tbsp. sugar
1 egg
⅔ cup milk

TOPPING:

⅓ cup BULK BISCUIT MIX
⅓ cup brown sugar
½ tsp. cinnamon

2 Tbsp. butter

Preheat oven to 400.

Grease 9-inch cake pan. Mix all ingredients well but do not over mix. Pour into greased pan. Mix topping ingredients until crumbly and spread evenly over top of batter. Bake about 20 minutes. Best served warm or room temperature.

EASY HOMEMADE SALISBURY STEAK AND GRAVY

I'VE BEEN MAKING these for quite a few years, and I never get tired of them. They're easy and not horrible nutritionally, but the best thing is they cook in the oven while you're doing something else. With a 5-minute prep time and a 35-minute cook time… Dinner's ready before you can say, "Please pass the bread."

Can be served over reheated, leftover mashed potatoes, bread, or even rice. This is a great fall or winter meal. Serves 2. Preheat oven to 350.

1 lb. hamburger
*2 cans vegetable **beef** soup**
(*this matters—vegetable beef soup with the little barleys in it)
¾ - 1 can water
½ tsp. onion powder
½ tsp. garlic powder
1 Tbsp. butter

Put the hamburger in a med. bowl and work it like you're making meatloaf or meatballs for 5-6 minutes. Then add in onion and garlic powders and work for another 2-3 minutes.

This will make the beef very firm when it cooks, and that's the goal.

Divide the hamburger in half and form two oblong shaped patties. Place them in a baking dish. Open the two cans of soup and spoon the contents over the meat. Pour the water into the pan. Cover tightly with foil.

Bake for 15 minutes then carefully pull back foil and stir, turn patties over, check to see if you need more water. You should have a thick soup in the pan, but you don't want to burn your pan, so a little water is needed. Replace foil and cook for another 20 minutes.

Remove the patties from the pan. Stir the butter into the pan and any remaining water while the pan is still hot. Using a potato masher, mash the soup contents. Pour over patties. This is wonderful gravy, and there's extra for mashed potatoes, rice, or even bread.

MAC AND TOM

THIS IS ONE of my very favorite frugal meals. I used to make it for my family, and I still make it occasionally for myself. My kids used to call it "welfare stew," I suppose because it uses so few ingredients, they must have decided that it was "poor people food." It is, as I said, a frugal meal... but it's delicious, filling, and has decent value as far as nutrition goes. I love it because it's frugal, quick to prepare, great for cold nights, and best of all— perfect for those nights you forgot to take something out of the freezer for dinner. You can cook frozen hamburger in the time it takes to boil the macaroni... Dinner in T-minus 20 minutes. Serves 4-6

3/4 of 1 lb. box of macaroni elbows, cooked

2 lg. cans of whole tomatoes

1 small can of diced tomatoes

1 ½ lbs. cooked hamburger

1 small onion

S+P

Garlic powder

Boil macaroni, drain, and set aside in kettle. Brown hamburger in pan with onion, S+ P, and garlic powder to taste. I put in about a tablespoon of garlic powder.

Open cans of tomatoes and mix with macaroni, turn heat on low. Before tomatoes heat up, use knife and potato masher to cut and mash them into bite sized pieces, allowing all of the juices to go into the pot with the pasta or you can squeeze them with your hands like I do. Remove any tomato cores you find.

When hamburger and onions are fully cooked, add them to the macaroni and tomatoes and stir. Heat thoroughly, then serve like soup. It should have a decent amount of juice in it.

This is one dish that is **not good** left over. The macaroni absorbs the juice, and turns to mush. So only make what you think you will use for one meal.

Excellent dish to have bread with and a perfect dish for cold nights!

QUICK AND EASY CHICKEN CUTLETS WITH POTATO WEDGES

THIS DINNER IS fast and thrifty. It takes a little prep work, and then it goes in the oven for a half an hour and magically comes out as a tasty meal for two. The pancake mix makes the coating on the chicken crispy, light and thick—

just the way I like it. Approximate price for two dinners? $2.50-$3.00. Preheat oven to 400F.

For chicken:

1 ½ - 2 cups dry pancake mix
1 egg mixed with 2 Tbsp. water
1 boneless chicken breast, butterfly cut, then halved.
S+P
1 tsp. Garlic powder
1 tsp. Old Bay seasoning
1 tsp. Paprika
1 tsp. lemon pepper
Cooking spray

For Potatoes:

2 medium potatoes, washed, with skin left on, cut into wedges
Salt and pepper to taste
Canola oil
Parsley

Put potato wedges in a bowl and drizzle with oil, season with S+P and parsley, and then work with your hands to coat all sides well. Once they are all coated, put them onto a sheet pan and into the oven, and then begin the chicken.

Once you have the chicken butterflied into two cutlets, season the egg mix with salt and pepper liberally. Mix the dry pancake mix with all of the seasonings. Spray a baking sheet with cooking spray.

Dredge the chicken in the pancake mix on both sides, then dip in the egg—then dredge again in the pancake mix and set aside on a plate for five minutes. Repeat for the other cutlet.

Check the potato wedges.

After the chicken has rested for 5 minutes, place on sprayed baking sheet and put in oven with potatoes. In 15 minutes, turn. By that time, the wedges will need to be turned as well.

By the 30-minute mark for chicken, both should be done and crispy. If not, allow another 5-8 minutes.

BREADED PORK TENDERLOIN MEDALLIONS W/ MASHED POTATOES

I BUY WHOLE pork tenderloins when they're on sale at my local grocery store at buy 1, get 1 free. For about $18, I get 2. I cut a couple of roasts and some 1-inch slices for these. I got 11 out of the half a tenderloin I sliced last night. This recipe also works beautifully with any cut of pork chop as well. Makes 10. Can be frozen.

1 egg
½ tsp. lemon juice
1 tsp. ground sage
Salt and pepper
2 Tbsp. water
1 ½ cups flour
1 Tbsp. lemon pepper
1 Tbsp. parsley
1 Tbsp. garlic powder

1 tsp. thyme
¼ tsp. salt
½ tsp. black pepper
½ tsp. ground sage
10 pork tenderloin medallions or 3 pork chops
6-7 potatoes
Oil for frying

Before you start with your pork, wash, peel and cut up your potatoes and put them on to boil. They will need a full 30 minutes and your pork will not take long, so plan accordingly.

Beat the egg, and then mix the rest of the ingredients in that group in a baking dish. In another baking dish, mix together the second list of ingredients.

Lay the pork in the egg mixture for about 30 minutes on each side to tenderize, and then as you bread it in the flour mixture, press down with the heel of your hand, flattening the pork. Flip and do the same to the other side. This will not only make your pork thinner so it will cook faster, but it also tenderizes it by breaking strands and fibers in the meat that might make it tough.

Once all of the pork has been coated in the flour, set it aside on a plate for at least 10 minutes to rest while you prepare a pan with oil for frying.

Check your potatoes.

Place pork in hot oil and cook until nicely browned, and then turn and do the same on the other side. Put pork in warm 250-degree oven to stay warm as you finish remainder. When done, check potatoes, drain, and mash according to how you like them and serve with your pork. A hearty dinner for fall will include some warmed applesauce.

I've taken the above pork to two barbecues now, and it disappears. The marinade tenderizes the meat and flavors it very well at the same time. Grilling it makes it even better. It's just as good cooked under your broiler in your oven too. Just don't overcook it. This is a good recipe for a tougher cut of pork or chicken, as it tenderizes so well.

MEATLESS BURGER ONE

2 cans white albacore tuna drained and rinsed
About ½ -¾ cup breadcrumbs 1 egg
½ tsp. onion powder flour for coating
1 Tbsp. minced onion oil for frying 1-2 Tbsp
½ tsp. garlic powder
¼ tsp. poultry seasoning
½ tsp. parsley
Pinch of salt and pepper

With a fork, shred tuna into tiny fragments. Mix in all other ingredients except flour and oil. With the right amount of breadcrumbs, patties should form easily. Mixture should be moist but not wet. If they are wet, add a bit more breadcrumbs. You should get two large burger sized patties.

Dip formed patties into flour to coat and then place in pan with heated oil. Fry on each side until golden brown. Serve on rolls with lettuce, tomato, onion—melt your favorite cheese over them. Enjoy your HEALTHY, INEXPENSIVE burgers! Most people will never know it's not beef.

MEATLESS BURGER TWO

(Vegetarian, not vegan—contains egg)

I AM A huge fan of beans. They're super cheap, really healthy, very versatile and, if you know how to cook them, extremely YUMMY! I have cooked beans all of my life, and created many dishes over the years—this one, an actual burger, makes me happy. I can eat it and not feel bad.

First, I'll tell you these are VERY filling, so make them smaller than you'd make a beef burger. Second, they freeze as well as beef burgers, so make extras. They're great topped with veggies and after they've been pan fried, they can be grilled easily.

1 cup cooked lentils
(You can use other beans too. I've used white northern a lot.)
1 egg
Crushed saltine crackers
Oil for frying
Garlic and onion powder to taste

Boil lentils in salted water until soft then strain with colander. When cooled, add egg and seasonings and enough cracker crumbs to form a patty. Place in hot oil. Cook until edges are brown and crisp, turn and cook on other side until browned and crisp.

LENTIL SOUP -VEGAN- NO ANIMAL PRODUCTS

I HAVE BEEN making lentil soup since I started cooking full time at fifteen years old. Lentils are very inexpensive, a huge source of protein, tasty and versatile. Lentil soup on an autumn or winter day with crusty bread will fill your stomach and your soul. If you wish to add some ham or any form of smoked pork, feel free, but this recipe is meatless and vegan, it contains no animal products... and it's delicious.

1 cup dry lentils
5 cups water
1 Tbsp. salt
⅛ tsp. thyme
⅛ tsp. Italian seasoning
1 large onion, diced
2 carrots, rough julienne
½ tsp. garlic powder
½ tsp. onion powder
¼ tsp. rosemary
2 stalks celery, rough chopped
¼ cup parsley
¼ cup canola oil
3 peeled, cubed potatoes
Additional water

Begin with a very hot 4 Qt. pan, heat canola oil in it... then drop in onion, celery, potatoes and carrots. Sauté quickly for 2-3 minutes then add seasonings and stir for 1-2 minutes until pan begins to brown on the bottom.

Add 5 cups of water and the lentils. Bring to a boil and cook for at least 2 hours. Add additional water as needed until lentils are soft and the soup is the thickness you prefer. Serve hot with bread or biscuits.

MARINATED PORK

2 cups pork cubes

¼ cup lemon juice

¼ cup canola oil

1 tsp. garlic powder

1 tsp. black pepper

½ tsp. ground sage

½ tsp. salt

2 Tbsp. vinegar

1 Tbsp. water

½ tsp. Worcestershire sauce

¼ cup Dijon mustard

Mix and marinate 4 hours before cooking. Mix all ingredients together in quart size zipper bag. Be sure they are well incorporated with the pork. Keep in refrigerator and allow marinating for at least 4 hours prior to cooking. Can also be used for chicken.

ITALIAN VEGETABLE SOUP

I MADE THIS for the first time when my youngest son was in the sixth grade. He was the only one home that fall weekend besides myself. I thought a nice soup and bread would be great for the two of us. My kids were accustomed to eating my soups and always loved them. This one was still in progress when John came downstairs and opened the kettle to peek. One look and he pronounced this soup a failure—that he wasn't eating it. I told him it wasn't done. He didn't care... hearing the ingredient list made him decide he wasn't eating it! A couple of hours later, the soup was done, and I was very happy with the results. I called up the stairs to my son and got no reply.

Soon, I heard the kettle lid rattle, and I knew he was getting himself some dinner. I'd had a bowlful in front of the TV since he took his time coming down. After one show was over, then another, I finally decided I'd better go put the leftover soup away and wash up the dishes.

I opened the kettle to find it nearly empty.

Because this was a soup that I was experimenting with, I didn't make a huge pot, but I made about three quarts. Now there was about an inch left in the bottom of my pot. Sheepishly, my son admitted he was wrong and confessed that my soup was really good. He'd eaten three large bowls.

It's very hearty and so nutritious!

3 lbs. stew meat or chuck roast (cut your own stew meat)

1 lg. onion

1 lg. can diced tomatoes with juice

1 tsp. garlic powder

1 tsp. parsley

Salt and pepper to taste

2 peeled Carrots—cut up into pieces

3 washed and peeled potatoes—cut into pieces

½ pkg. frozen broccoli

½ pkg. frozen cauliflower

1 small zucchini

1 small can mushrooms

Handful of celery

½ tsp. basil

½ tsp. paprika

1 Tbsp. flour

¾ cup very small pasta—or elbow macaroni—COOKED

Put oil in your pan and turn the heat on med-high. Toss in cut up onions, potatoes, and carrots. Fry and lightly brown. Add S&P, mushrooms, and meat with garlic once potatoes and carrots begin to brown up. Sauté meat, getting it nice and brown. Toss in a bit of flour—1 TBSP—this will add flavor and color to broth after. Keep stirring with heat on med-high. Add in remainder of seasonings, celery, and tomatoes. Once tomatoes are in, scrape and stir well, getting all bits from the bottom. This is called deglazing, and it's what makes your gravy, soup broth, spaghetti sauce, etc. wonderful... those beautiful little brown fried bits of flavor need to be *unstuck* from your pan, and incorporated into your dish... So... we just did that.... with liquid. That's how you do it. Otherwise, you deglaze them right into your dishwater later… and that doesn't make your meal taste good, does it?

Bring this all to a good boil then add about 6 cups of water. Put a lid on, turn it down, and let this cook for at least one hour at a good simmer, until the potatoes and carrots are soft.

Okay... Now, zucchini, broccoli, and cauliflower are left. Toss those in and let the pot simmer another half hour. Toss in the cooked pasta during the last five minutes. If you'd like, you can add one can of white beans now too—drain and rinse them before adding.

The beef will be tender, the veggies flavorful, and the broth very satisfying. This isn't your mama's soup... this is soup that made a sixth-grade boy change his mind about soup

THE GREAT THING about this recipe is that it can be prepared easily for on or three or five. I love that about it. I make it quite a bit for myself. It's Lasagna with a fancy, upscale twist... Fresh mozzarella makes it so much better than the bagged kind. This meal is just a nice, adult treat... and with my frugal tweaks to the recipe, it's pretty inexpensive for one or two people. I don't miss the fresh basil or tomatoes—the canned ones work! Another thing, sometimes I just don't want a lot of leftovers for the freezer, so this is perfect.

LASAGNA ROLL UPS

8 lasagna noodles
¾ cup ricotta cheese
⅓ cup parmesan cheese
1 lg. can whole tomatoes, sliced
14 oz. fresh mozzarella cheese
1 egg
¼ cup basil
marinara sauce
Preheat oven to 350

Cook lasagna noodles per instructions on box and drain them. Lay out on non-stick surface. Mix ricotta and egg until well blended then stir in parmesan. Place this on each noodle from end to end. Cover the ricotta with slices of tomato. Then top the tomatoes with the slices of fresh mozzarella. Sprinkle basil on top.

Snugly roll each noodle to the other end.

Spread about ½ cup marinara sauce in bottom of baking dish (11x7)

Put lasagna rolls seam side down. Cover each with 2 TBSP of marinara sauce. BE SURE TO COVER EDGES. Sprinkle top of each roll with parmesan cheese and 1 slice of mozzarella. Bake 30 minutes.

THIS CAN BE a very inexpensive meal if you buy your peppers at the farmer's market or even in the stores when they're in season. The rest of the time, here in NY, unless you're only buying two or so, forget it—you could eat steak cheaper. For real. These freeze and travel really well, are nutritious, and I just love them in the fall. You can also core, blanch, and freeze just the peppers to stuff later.

These are one of my favorite things to freeze and have for those nights I may not want to cook. That's why this recipe makes so many. I've also made fewer peppers, and the same amount of everything else, and used the filling as a side—Spanish rice. Versatility, people… if you can be flexible and creative, you'll never be hungry.

STUFFED PEPPERS

Preheat oven to 350 degrees.
1 lb. hamburger
½ cup raw white rice
4-6 bell peppers
1 cup water
2- 8 oz. cans tomato sauce
1 Tbsp. Worcestershire Sauce
¼ tsp. garlic powder
¼ tsp. onion powder
S+P to taste
1 tsp. Italian seasonings

Put rice and water in pan—bring to a boil, cover and cook 20 minutes. Brown hamburger. Clean peppers by removing tops and seeds, wash outsides well. Mix hamburger, cooked rice, 1 can of sauce, Worcestershire sauce, garlic and onion powders in bowl—season with S+P. Spoon mixture into each pepper, filling nearly to top.

Mix remaining can of sauce with Italian seasoning and pour over the top of all of the now stuffed peppers. Bake COVERED for 1 hour, basting with the tomato sauce every 15 minutes until the peppers are tender and no longer crunchy.

LO MEIN

THE FUNNY THING about this dish is that for years, I wouldn't eat it. I wouldn't even try it. I thought it must be disgusting with all of those "things" in there. Then, one day, I surprisingly tried it. I was hooked from then on! Every time I went to the Chinese restaurant after that, I had to have Lo Mein, whether house, vegetable, pork, beef or shrimp... I didn't care. I love them all. At home, I make the vegetable for a side dish to use up leftover veggies, and I make pork and beef with small pieces of meats leftover from trimming ribs and roasts or tenderloin ends.

With stir-fry and Lo Mein, plus soups and such—there's no reason a veggie or meat should ever go unused. Here's my recipe, but you can add what you like too.

½ lb. cooked spaghetti, soaked in soy sauce mixture, and ready
¼ cup chopped onion
¼ cup chopped bell pepper of your choice
½ cup frozen or fresh broccoli
¼ cup chopped celery
Mushrooms

Meat, that's been marinated for 2-3 hours in same mixture as spaghetti, but separately. If you choose to add meat.

½ cup frozen or fresh green beans

Oil for frying- 1-2 Tbsp.

¼ tsp. garlic powder

¼ tsp. ground ginger

Makes 4-5 one cup servings

Two to three hours ahead, prepare and cool ½ lb. spaghetti, drain, and place in bowl with a ½ cup soy sauce, 2 Tbsp. brown sugar, and ½ tsp. ground ginger. Cover and place in refrigerator until you're ready to prepare your Lo Mein. Save this sauce.

Same for your meat, if you're using it, cut it into ½ inch by ½ inch chunks. Before putting it into its own bowl of the soy sauce mixture.

When you're ready, chop all of your veggies, drain the sauce from your meat, and discard it. Drain the sauce from your spaghetti and save it nearby. Pour 1-2 Tbsp. of oil into a skillet and allow it to heat well. When it's hot, add meat first and toss until all edges are browned, then add in all of the veggies. As veggies are sautéing, add a Tbsp. or so of the soy sauce mixture at a time until you've added 3-5 tablespoons and the veggies are the way you like them. I like mine almost done with little-to-no crunch. Some prefer theirs nearly raw. Cook them how you like. Then toss in the spaghetti you marinated. Stir it around until it's heated through well. Add in garlic powder and ground ginger. Toss and serve.

STIR FRY

I STARTED MAKING my own stir-fry to use up leftover meat and vegetables. Of course, I like it, but I was more thrilled to have found a use for those things that wasn't soup or stew. I only buy pork tenderloin when it is buy one, get one free at my local Tops Market. I cut it up myself into a couple of small roasts, pork medallions, and the sloppy, messed up ends and pieces. You got it—they become Pork Stir Fry. I also trim my pork ribs when I'm portioning them, and those pieces go into my stir-fry, as well. Ditto for beef roasts. I have large sized zipper bags in my freezer that I have labeled and can add to and remove from as needed, because everything is individually wrapped. One is for veggies and the other is for meats. I have celery, carrots, peppers, celery leaves, and whole baby carrots right now in my veg bag. My meat bag contains three slices of thick sliced bacon. This makes is so nice for when I have a bit of whatever leftover, I can toss it in there. It's perfect for the next Stir Fry or Lo Mein... or even spaghetti sauce. I'm so glad I moved beyond saving all of those things for JUST soup. BUT, I still want my Lo Mein and my Stir Fry to be what they've always been to me. I don't want them to have things in them they normally don't when I buy them prepared. So, this is how I make my Stir Fry.

1 ½ cups chopped meat of your choice:
chicken, beef, or pork in ½ cup soy sauce
2 Tbsp. brown sugar
½ tsp. ginger for at least 2-3 hours, in the refrigerator in a covered dish

Prepare rice by boiling 1 ½ cups water and ¾ cup rice.
Cook until water is absorbed and rice is tender.

About ¼ cup each:
mushrooms
onions

cauliflower

thin sliced carrots

bell peppers

broccoli

celery

Make a sauce of ½ cup soy sauce, 2 Tbsp. brown sugar and 1/2 tsp. ground ginger. Set aside. Heat pan on stove and add a Tbsp. of oil. Be sure pan is hot and begin cooking meat. DISCARD THE MARINADE FROM THE MEAT. Cook the meat fast and move it around, browning it. Add in a Tbsp. of flour and quickly stir.

Add all vegetables together, unless you've added some that are harder, like sweet potatoes. Add those first and let cook a bit before adding the others. Pour in the sauce you set aside. Add some good heat and in 3-4 minutes, your vegetables will be slightly crunchy and your meat will be done. Pour meat and veggie stir-fry over your cooked rice and serve.

EATING WELL AND eating frugally are not hard. It's about choices and taking advantage of opportunities to save when you see them. Sometimes, the choice to save on one thing means the opportunity to splurge on something else. It's nice to have some of the better things in life, but not all of us can splurge on them. Meals like this one will make you feel as if you're not missing a thing.

MOCK LINGUINE WITH WHITE CLAM SAUCE—NO CLAMS

1 can of chicken breast
½ cup chicken stock
¼ cup butter
¼ cup your favorite oil
1 Tbsp. flour
½ tsp. garlic powder
½ Tbsp. parsley
¼ tsp. basil
½ lb. Linguine pasta
Black pepper to taste
½ cup evaporated milk

Cook Linguine in boiling water and then drain and set aside. In a large saucepan, combine canned chicken breast, chicken stock, and remainder of ingredients and place over med. heat. Cook until boiling. Add ½-cup evaporated milk and cook until sauce begins to thicken. Remove from heat and pour over linguine. Serve hot with crusty bread. Serves 2

Try substituting imitation crab or imitation lobster for the chicken.

PIZZA ZITI

THIS BEATS PLAIN old baked ziti any day! Which is what I *was* about to make until this deliciousness happened. I made extra on purpose and put single servings in the freezer. They taste even better now. My grandson Michael, a very picky eater, even ate this… so if he eats it, it must be good.

I had pepperoni, meatballs, and sausage in my freezer. I like meat lover's pizza. I already had hamburger out for baked ziti, added some mushrooms and onions, and this dish became my dream pizza that quick! I just had to simmer my sauce a bit longer because of some ingredients being frozen. No problem. Plain old baked ziti? Never again.

1 box of ziti
1 onion
1 lb. of hamburger
1 lb. of sweet or hot sausage
1 tsp. Italian seasoning or oregano
6 oz. of pepperoni slices- cut in half
1 lg. jar spaghetti sauce
1 can mushrooms
1-2 C shredded mozzarella or blended cheese
Any other "pizza" toppings you like
Cooking spray

Cook ziti to your preferred doneness, remembering that it's going to go into the oven for another 10-15 minutes. Drain and set aside. Spray large ovenproof pan with cooking spray. Preheat oven to 400.

Cook onion, hamburger, sausage, and Italian seasoning over medium heat in Dutch oven until browned and done. Season with salt and pepper. Add in mushrooms then stir in jar of sauce and pepperoni. Simmer on low until heated thoroughly and then stir in ziti.

At this time, you should have all of your pizza toppings and pasta cooked and mixed—except the cheese.

Pour mixture into your baking pan, then top with the cheese and bake until cheese is melted and browned.

I STARTED MAKING this chicken when my kids were young and asking for trips to fast food restaurants for chicken nuggets. With a family of six then, a McDinner out was $40 or more, with no leftovers and nothing nutritionally sound in little bellies. I was certain I could come up with nuggets that would make them happy and not break my strained budget.

It took some work. For many years, I had to buy chicken thighs and debone them myself to save on the cost. My kids loved this, and we never really had a name for it. The kids just knew it took me a lot of time and work... so we didn't have it more than once a week or so. They started calling it my "special chicken" and it stuck. Someone would ask what was for dinner, I'd reply "chicken" and they'd get all excited and ask, "Your *SPECIAL* chicken??" Then I'd say no and see a small, dejected face... and try to placate them with shake and bake chicken. It didn't really work. They loved my special chicken and I was happy about that, happy I'd found a way to make nuggets at home, happy my kids were happy, even if they were dark meat. White meat was too expensive, and boneless white meat was out of the question.

By the time most of the kids had left home, boneless breasts could be had for $2.99/lb. That was a deal then, so I sometimes splurged on those. What a treat not to have all that deboning prep time! I also didn't need to buy as much by then, so it didn't break the bank. Now I buy boneless breasts for myself. Of course, only when they're on sale and today on sale is $1.99/lb. or less. I often get them for buy one, get one free. Two packages cost me about $12 and I get eight whole breasts, which I halve. Sixteen meals of meat for $12. Even as adults my kids still hold my "special" chicken dear. It brings back great memories for me. I never wrote this recipe down until just a couple of months ago. I suppose it's time to pass it on.

This chicken is great cold as leftovers and makes a terrific chicken sandwich with mayo too!

MAMA'S "SPECIAL CHICKEN"

Boneless chicken
Oil for frying
Flour
Breadcrumbs
1 egg + 3 Tbsp. milk beaten together

All measurements from here to end need to be equal—if you use ½ tsp. of one spice, use the same for all.

Garlic powder
Onion powder
Poultry seasoning
Salt
Pepper
Parsley
Parmesan cheese

Cut chicken into strips or nuggets, whichever shape suits you. Have a bowl of flour, a bowl of egg mixture, and a bowl that contains HALF flour and HALF breadcrumbs. Into the breadcrumbs and flour mix, add EQUAL measures of each seasoning.

Example: If you add ½ tsp. of garlic powder, add ½ tsp. of each of the other spices too so they're all the same. Use your own taste. Once all seasonings are added, mix well.

Dip the chicken in flour first, then in egg mixture, and last, in seasoned breadcrumbs with flour.

NOTE: As chicken pieces are in the last mixture, press down with the heel of your hand. Your strips or nuggets will flatten, thin out, and cook super-fast. This also breaks up any tough fibers and tenderizes them.

Fry in oil on both sides, quickly drain, and put in 200-degree oven to keep warm while you fry the remainder. Serve with dipping sauce of your choice.

If you'd like these to be spicy, add 1 tsp. cayenne and 1 tsp. extra of black pepper to your flour and breadcrumb mixture.

CHIPPED BEEF IN WHITE SAUCE

WHEN I TELL my boys I'm making this for dinner, they suck in a happy breath. My oldest always asks me to make plenty and if I made it three times a week, they'd be thrilled. I call it meat sauce over toast. They call it S.O.S. and always make it a point to tell me what that stands for in the navy. I prefer the term meat sauce, thank you. Either way, it's cheap, filling, not *terribly* unhealthy, and one of their favorites.

I always use homemade bread. Store bought bread requires four, sometimes six slices of toast to fill these boys up. With homemade, two fat slices will do. I catch the sliced deli meat packs on sale for less than three dollars and freeze two or three of them. Start by making a basic white sauce. *Get to know this white sauce. It comes in handy for all kinds of other dishes.*

Here's how I make it.

1 lb. pre-packaged shaved ham (It's near the sliced cheese and hot dogs) chopped into small pieces.

5 Tbsp. butter

1/4 cup flour

6 cups milk

Garlic salt, pepper, seasoning salt to taste
Homemade bread, toasted

Melt the butter in a big pot. Add the flour and whisk it until it looks like this.

Then add 2 cups of milk. Keep on medium heat and whisk the lumps out. It might start to thicken up, and that's fine. Add the other four cups of milk and the spices and whisk. This will look very watery and you'll think you are whisking forever and nothing is happening. Sometimes, it takes ten minutes or so. Keep on medium heat, keep stirring, and it will thicken up. It's okay if it boils. Just be sure to scrape the bottom so it doesn't scald. When it looks almost thick enough, add the chopped meat and stir some more. A few more minutes and it will be ready to ladle over toast. I make a lot of broccoli because that's one of the few vegetables the entire family will eat. So while I was making the white sauce, I had broccoli steaming. Total prep time is around 20 minutes.

The price breakdown is this:
$3.00: Shaved lunchmeat
$1.00: Milk
$1.00: Broccoli (I buy big bags of frozen that last 4-5 meals)
Total: $5.00

You could drive it down even more using powdered milk, using canned veggies, or catching an even better shaved meat sale.

This white sauce is the base for a lot of other recipes. It's extremely versatile and it is the frugal cook's friend. Learn it. Love it. You will see it again.

SIMPLE SOUPS USING POTATO FLAKES

THIS IS EXTREMELY versatile. You can custom make several creations.

1 onion chopped or 2 Tbsp. onion flakes
1 garlic clove minced or garlic salt to taste
2 Tbsp. butter
4 cups milk
1 ½ cups instant mashed potato flakes
1 ½ tsp. salt
¼ tsp. pepper

Combine all ingredients in a saucepan. Heat to nearly boiling stirring constantly. Remove from heat. Sprinkle with shredded cheddar cheese and serve.

Variation: Add cooked chopped ham, bacon, or bacon bits, or ½ pound of cooked ground beef. Peas and/or carrots go well in this. Corn and celery would go well with a cup of chopped chicken or turkey. Get creative! This is a great recipe to use leftover meat and veggies from the week.

POT PIES (HAND PIES)

Piecrust
Your choice of meat
Your choice of veggies
3 potatoes
Garlic salt, season salt, onion flakes (any seasoning you prefer)
2-3 cups of poultry or brown gravy.
For this recipe, you'll make your own piecrust first.
1 cup shortening or lard
2 ⅔ cups flour
1 tsp. salt
7-8 Tbsp. cold water

Blend the flour, salt, and shortening until the mixture resembles coarse crumbs. Stir in water a Tbsp. at a time until mixture forms a ball. Divide dough into about 12 small balls.

You'll want to make a meat and veggie mixture to go inside. Hamburger, potatoes, and peas are our favorites. I brown ¾ lb. hamburger, peel and dice 3 potatoes, and add 1 can of peas. Add onion flakes, 1 tsp. garlic salt, 1 tsp. seasoned salt, ½ tsp. pepper or any spice combination your family likes. Mix together in a large bowl. You can use any meat and veggie combination you want, including or excluding the potatoes. Though the potatoes really do make for more pies.

Roll each ball out to a 6 to 8-inch circle. Place a heaping half cup of your meat/potato/veggie mixture on one side. Pull the dough over and pinch the sides to seal. Place on a greased cookie sheet. Repeat until you've used all the dough and/or meat mixture.

Bake at 400 for 25-30 minutes. Use a sharp knife to poke through and test if the potatoes are soft.

Let cool five minutes. Use poultry or brown gravy depending on your meat. Transfer the meat pies to dinner plates and pour gravy over the top.

This can just as easily convert to a pot pie by placing one rolled out crust in a pie pan, adding your meat/veggie mixture and half the gravy. Top with another piecrust, pinch the edges and make a few cuts to let out steam.

Bake a full pie at 400 for 35-45 minutes. Plate each hand pie, pour gravy over the top, and serve.

QUICK AND EASY ALFREDO SAUCE

½ cup butter
8 oz. cream cheese
1 tsp. garlic powder
2 cups milk
6 oz. parmesan cheese
Dash of pepper

Melt butter, add cream cheese, and garlic powder. Whisk until smooth. Stir in parmesan cheese and pepper. Cook on medium heat until thickened. Add chopped chicken and pour over cooked egg noodles.

GOULASH

PERFECT FOR COLD winter nights. And again, highly customizable. Add whatever vegetables you like, use ground chicken instead of beef, and adjust spices to your liking. Leave out the tomatoes and use a few cups of beef broth instead. You can add elbow noodles during the last hour of cooking if you wish. Here's the way I make it. (I am guesstimating at the amount of seasonings because this is truly a throw-it-together kind of dinner.)

1 lb. ground beef, fried and drained
2 large potatoes, peeled and diced
1 can green beans
1 can corn
1 can peas and carrots
1 can tomato sauce
1 can diced tomatoes, drained
Seasonings

After browning the ground beef, put it in the Crock-Pot and add all other ingredients.
Add:
1 tsp. garlic salt
1 tsp. Italian seasoning
2 tsp. seasoned salt
1 tsp. pepper
½ tsp. marjoram
½ tsp. thyme.

Set Crock-Pot on high for 3-4 hours. Serve with homemade bread or biscuits.

HAM FRIED RICE

THIS IS GOOD for a side or a dish. My boys like it when I make a big batch and keep it in the fridge for them to dip into when they feel snacky.

8-10 eggs, scrambled
½ cup milk
2 cups rice
½ -1 lb. ham, chopped fine
Carrots, diced (optional)
Peas, drained (optional)
Garlic salt
Seasoned salt
Soy sauce

Cook two cups of rice with whatever method you prefer. Stove top, rice cooker, etc. While the rice is cooking, scramble the eggs, mix in milk, and cook in a skillet. When the rice is done, add the cooked scrambled eggs, diced ham, and veggies of your choice. Mix well. Add a dash of garlic salt and seasoned salt. Sprinkle with soy sauce to taste. Some like a little soy, others like it drenched. I sprinkle lightly and let others add more to their bowl. Serve right away or keep covered in the refrigerator. Will stay good 2-3 days.

EASY BEAN SOUP

MADE FROM CANNED baked beans, or even your own leftover ones, this soup is hearty and full of nutrition. Toss in some leftover ham if you have some, at the end. It can stand alone with just some warm homemade bread, or pair it with Molly's hand pies if you're feeding a real hungry crowd. I love the simplicity of this soup, how easy it is to make, and how available all of the ingredients are. Not everyone has the time to soak dried beans overnight and boil them all day. With this recipe, anyone on any budget, with any schedule, can enjoy a good bean soup. Perfect.

4 cups canned or cooked baked beans—pureed
2 cans (small size) stewed tomatoes
1 bay leaf
1 Tbsp. parsley
1 cup sliced carrots
1 cup sliced celery
½ cup sliced onions
1 cup sliced, peeled potatoes
2 qts. water
2 tsp. salt
1 tsp. cumin (optional)

Combine bean puree, tomatoes, bay leaf, and parsley. Cook remaining veggies until just tender in as little water as possible. Combine bean mixture, vegetables, 2 qts. of water and salt. Simmer 1 hr. Serve hot. Serves 6

CHICKEN AND DUMPLINGS

THIS RECIPE IS easy and frugal and was always a staple meal in my home when my kids were growing up. I still make it now, just on a smaller scale. It's a fall and winter meal that warms the belly and pleases the soul.

1 onion, roughly chopped
2 stalks of celery, leaves and all, roughly chopped
2 carrots, julienne chopped
8 chicken thighs
1 bay leaf
½ tsp. thyme
½ tsp. rosemary
1 tsp. lemon juice
½ tsp. parsley
1 tsp. poultry seasoning
Oil

DUMPLINGS:

1 cup flour
1 ½ tsp. baking powder
½ tsp. salt
1 tsp. parsley
1 egg
½ cup milk

Heat oil in Dutch oven style pan on stove. Season chicken thighs well with salt and pepper then put into pan skin side down. Add onions, celery, and carrots. Stir around and allow vegetables and chicken to brown, but not burn, turning chicken as needed. When the chicken is browned, and the vegetables have some color on them, add water to deglaze the pan, enough until the chicken is covered, and put in the seasonings, as well. Cover with a lid and simmer for at least one hour or more.

When your chicken is done, check to see if you need to add water again. Make sure that water is at least 3 inches above the chicken so that your dumplings will have room to cook.

Mix the dry ingredients for the dumplings. Bring pot to a boil. Add eggs and milk to dumpling mixture. Mix ONLY until moistened. Do not over mix. Drop dumplings into pot by the tablespoon so they don't touch. Cover tightly and let simmer gently for 20 minutes. Don't open the lid. Makes 4 servings.

CORN CHOWDER

IN THE NORTHEAST, you can walk into anyone's house on the weekend for a visit, and they will either be making corn chowder or ladling it from a pot into storage bowls because they've just finished dinner. Corn chowder is as northeast as a Boston accent. Easy, economical, and tasty—yeah, we Northeasterners know how to eat.

4 slices bacon
2 large onions, diced
3-4 Potatoes, peeled and diced
½ cup water
4 cups corn, cut fresh from the cob
1 qt. milk
2 ¼ tsp. salt
⅛ tsp. pepper

In a Dutch oven type pan, fry bacon until crisp, do not drain bacon drippings out. Then add in onions and cook until browned. Add potatoes and water. Simmer for 15 minutes.

Add the corn in that you have cut off the cob, making sure to also add in any juices from it. Simmer another 5-8 minutes until corn and potatoes are tender. Stir in milk and salt and pepper, heating slowly until chowder is piping hot. Makes 6-8 servings

THE EASIEST CHICKEN AND DUMPLINGS. EVER.

I GREW UP watching my grandmother make this. It would be a half day affair starting with her boiling a chicken, deboning, simmering the seasonings in the broth and then rolling out dumpling dough to make thin squares. She would painstakingly cut and drop the squares into the boiling broth so they didn't stick together. I still use the simplicity of her recipe but not so much the detail. This can be made relatively quickly. As I said, I cook and debone chicken in large quantities and then store in baggies in the freezer ahead of time so that is taken care of.

I add about 8 cups of water to a large pot and season to taste.

I use garlic salt, onion salt, season salt, pepper, garlic and 4 Tbsp. chicken bouillon or chicken soup base. This recipe is scalable. If you are making lunch for one, use two cups of water and fewer dumplings. Double it for a bigger crowd. The chicken (about a cup and a half) is precooked so I toss that in and bring it to a boil.

While it's simmering on medium heat, I mix the dumplings. I put 3 cups of flour into a bowl and add just enough milk to make a stiff, slightly sticky dough. Just add a little milk at a time until you get it easy to handle. It looks something like this.

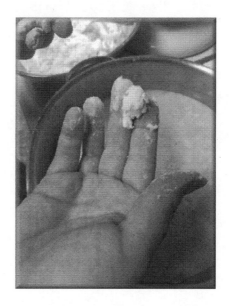

I turn up the simmering broth to near boiling. Then I pinch off small balls of dough and drop it in. One after another, just drop it in. Stop and stir every few minutes and you'll see it will start to thicken. You will either use all the dough or stop adding dumplings because the broth is looking full.

Sometimes, I'll add cooked (or canned) carrots to this, and if I add celery, I'll do it at the very beginning so it can soften. This, like so many of the recipes I use, is just a foundation for you to create something unique to your tastes.

SKILLET MEALS

HAMBURGER HELPER HACKS

I like this recipe because not only does it taste really good and it has no preservatives or coloring, it's also a fast dinner.

I use 3/4 lb. of hamburger for anything that calls for a pound. I get more dinners that way. Trust me, no one will notice. Comparing the box mix to the homemade version, you can make this for about $0.20. (I even buy elbow noodles in bulk so your mileage may vary.)

Here's the recipe and then I'll discuss a further time-saving hack.

SKILLET DINNER: BEEFY NOODLE

3/4 - 1 lb. hamburger
1 tsp. onion powder or flakes (I prefer flakes)
1 tsp. parsley
1 Tbsp. cornstarch
1/2 tsp. garlic powder (or salt)
1/2 tsp. salt (I use Himalayan pink salt for a mineral boost)
1 tsp. sugar
1/4 tsp. pepper
1 tsp. beef base (bouillon might work, too. Play with it.)
Dash of seasoning salt. (personal touch, feel free to omit.)
2 cups milk

1 cup water

1 cup elbow noodles

Brown the hamburger, drain and add everything else. Cook over medium heat until the noodles are soft and the sauce thickens up. Exact same way you make the box mix.

Here's a further time saver hack. You can measure out all the spices and noodles and store them in a jar or baggie. Then, it truly is just as convenient as the box.

While dinner was simmering, I went ahead and prepped three more to put on the shelf. Another dinner for less than five dollars. Bread is homemade and corn was frozen, bought in bulk.

SKILLET DINNER: CHILI MAC

¾ - 1 lb. ground beef (or ground chicken, turkey)
2 ¼ cup hot water
½ cup milk
1 cup elbow macaroni
1 can stewed tomatoes, drained (optional)

Sauce packet:
1 Tbsp. cornstarch
1 Tbsp. chili powder
1 tsp. onion powder
1 tsp. garlic
1 tsp. salt
1 tsp. sugar
1 cup shredded cheddar cheese

Brown the ground meat. Add water, milk, tomatoes, pasta, and spices. Bring to a boil. Cook on medium heat stirring often until thickened and pasta is tender. Remove from heat and stir in cheese, reserving some cheese to sprinkle on top before serving.

SKILLET DINNER: LASAGNA HELPER

1 lb. ground beef (or ground chicken, turkey)
2 ¼ cups hot water

½ cup milk

1 ½ cup small egg noodles or mini lasagna noodles

1 cup stewed or diced tomatoes, drained

Sauce packet:

1 Tbsp. cornstarch

1 Tbsp. mixed Italian herbs

1 tsp. onion powder

1 tsp. garlic

1 tsp. salt

1 tsp. sugar.

1-2 cups shredded mozzarella cheese

Brown the ground meat. Add water, milk, tomatoes, pasta, and spices. Bring to a boil. Cook on medium heat stirring often until thickened and pasta is tender. Remove from heat and stir in cheese.

SKILLET DINNER: BEEF TACO WITH CHEESE

1 pound ground beef (or ground chicken, turkey)

2 1/4 cups hot water

1/2 cup milk

1 cup rice

1 8 oz. can stewed or diced tomatoes, drained

Sauce packet:

1 Tbsp. cornstarch

1 package taco seasoning

1 tsp. onion powder

1 tsp. garlic

1 tsp. salt

1 tsp. sugar.

1 -1 ½ cups shredded cheddar cheese

1-2 cups shredded mozzarella cheese

Brown the ground meat. Add water, milk, tomatoes, rice, and spices. Bring to a boil. Cook on medium heat stirring often until thickened and rice is tender. Remove from heat and stir in most of the cheese, reserving some to sprinkle on top. Serve alone or with corn chips.

FRENCH DIPS WITH AU JUS

START BY USING the hot dog bun recipe to create hoagie buns. Divide the dough into 8 to make bigger buns.

You can make the meat for French dips two ways. If there is a good sale on roast beef, use that. Otherwise, use hamburger.

For roast beef, chop the meat and sauté it in butter with onion, garlic salt, and seasoned salt. If using hamburger, shape the meat into long, thin patties to fit the bun, sprinkle with the spices above, and fry.

While the meat is cooking, make your own Au Jus dipping sauce by adding 2 cups of water, 1 Tbsp. beef bouillon granules, ¼ tsp. pepper, ¼ tsp. crushed red pepper, and ¼ tsp. garlic salt to a saucepan. Bring to a boil and then keep warm while the meat finishes cooking. Transfer the meat to the buns and the Au Jus to a dipping bowl. This is fantastic with a side salad and Daisy's Parmesan potato wedges.

FAST CHICKEN PARMESAN

They make a cheap chicken parmesan box dinner that tastes like salt and cardboard. It wasn't hard to figure out how to make it myself for less money and a bit healthier. It still uses Banquet chicken patties, but, as I've said, we aren't perfect in our eating. It's another dinner that is under five dollars, better than fast food, and perfect for a busy night. It can easily be made ahead and frozen. Even the instructions are simple.

Arrange two chicken patties per person in a baking dish. Cover with a jar of spaghetti sauce. (I use home canned, but you can use anything store bought as well.) Top with parmesan cheese and/or mozzarella cheese. Bake at 350 for about a half an hour. The patties are pre-cooked, so you're only heating them up and allowing the cheese to broil. I have pre-made this in casserole pans and frozen as well.

Mashed potatoes and Italian don't really go together, but my bread was still in the oven so we sort of mixed it up. Peas were canned in this dinner. I'm having a hard time finding bulk frozen peas, even at Costco. I shall keep searching!

CREAMED TUNA

2 cans of Tuna in water, drained
2 cans cream of mushroom soup
1 can of milk (using empty soup can)
Spices to taste. (garlic salt, pepper, season salt, etc)

Mix all ingredients together. Heat on the stovetop on medium heat. Serve over toast, rice, or noodles. Adding peas or carrots is optional.

EVERYBODY KNOWS PORK chops and applesauce go together...like… well, pork chops and applesauce. So what happens when you're making pork chops and you have no applesauce, and no apples to make applesauce either…? Six minutes until pork chops are done, you do what I did. You make a sauce that TASTES like applesauce... out of apple JUICE. Tastes amazing on vanilla ice cream too!

APPLE JUICE SAUCE FOR PORK CHOPS

1 ½ cups apple juice

½ tsp. cinnamon

¼ tsp. ground cloves

¼ tsp. allspice

½ cup raisins

½ cup powdered sugar

2 Tbsp. cornstarch, mixed with water

Put all ingredients except cornstarch mixture in med. pan on stove. Bring to low boil and stir frequently for about 5 minutes then bring to fast boil. Stir in cornstarch and continue to stir as sauce thickens. About 2-3 minutes. Remove from heat and allow sauce to cool slightly before pouring over pork. Refrigerate leftovers and use within 3-5 days. This sauce is somewhat thin. If you prefer a thicker sauce, more like a gravy, increase the cornstarch mixture.

CASSEROLES

CASSEROLES ARE VERY simple, all-in-one dishes. You really don't need a lot of recipes for them because they are so easy to create. We have added several here, but just know that all you need for a casserole is a meat, a starch (rice, pasta, or potatoes), soup or homemade white sauce, a vegetable and spices.

Combine your meat, vegetables and starch in a casserole dish. Over it, pour a cream of mushroom, cream of chicken or a white sauce that you've made. Add spices and stir. Maybe add cheese. Or sour cream. Get creative. I generally bake casseroles at 350 for up to an hour. It depends on if your starch is pre-cooked or not.

TACO TOT CASSEROLE

HERE'S ANOTHER ONE that is good to make several of and freeze. In a frying pan, brown ¾ lb. hamburger. Add 1 packet taco seasoning and ¾ cup water. Add 1 can of refried beans and mix well. Cook and let thicken for 5 minutes. Pour into a casserole dish and layer the top with tater tots or chopped potatoes. Adding a can of drained, diced tomatoes and olives is optional. Sprinkle cheddar cheese on top and bake at 350 for 45 minutes.

If baking from frozen, add 15 minutes to the cook time. Top with sour cream when serving.

HAM AND CHEESE CASSEROLE

THIS LAST SUNDAY was so busy. Hubby and I were running hard from the second cup of coffee until Game of Thrones came on that night. (Everything stops for GOT.) I needed a quick dinner and dessert. Luckily, I had one in the freezer so I could just pop it in the oven while I threw together the cake.

This is one of my all-time favorites. I buy one ham a month and divide it up for a variety of meals. When I started making this, I realized I wanted to make extra because it freezes and reheats so well.

Two things you should know:

This will make a large batch—at least two 6x9 casseroles. I have been known to double this again and put three casseroles in the freezer.

It's pretty hard to screw this up. In fact, I never even measure when I make this anymore but dug out the original recipe to post here. It's truly a homemade convenience food for a fraction of the cost. It doesn't get any cheesier than this.

Here's how to do it.

8 oz. macaroni (elbow noodles)
1-2 cup diced ham
1/4 cup butter
1/4 cup flour
4 cups milk
1 tsp. salt
Dash of pepper
Dash of season salt
8 oz. shredded cheddar cheese
(I never measure. I throw in 3 handfuls—sometimes four.)

Boil elbow noodles, drain, and set aside. In a large saucepan, melt the butter and add the flour, salt, pepper, and any other spices you like. It will be lumpy. That's fine. Stir in 2 cups of milk and whisk until mostly smooth. Add remaining milk and stir frequently on medium heat until it starts to thicken. Scrape the bottom often to avoid scorching. Add cheese and stir until melted. It will thicken even more after you add the cheese.

Throw in the ham and the cooked noodles and mix well. You can add veggies here if you like. Peas go nicely in this. If you like onions, sauté them when you first melt the butter.

Pour into two medium casserole dishes. Bake one at 375° for 20 minutes. Cover the second and freeze. To reheat from frozen, I heat at 325° for about an hour.

CHICKEN CASSEROLE

2 lbs. chicken

(You can use leftover chicken, canned or boiled from fryers)

2 cans cream of mushroom soup

1 cup sour cream

2 chicken bouillon, crumbled

2 cans vegetables, (your choice) drained.

1 cup milk

1-2 boxes of stuffing

Seasoning to taste.

(I use some garlic salt, seasoning salt and onion flakes)

This can make several casseroles depending on the size of your family. Mix chicken, soup, sour cream, vegetables, bouillon, and milk together. Place in 1-2 oiled casserole pans.

Prepare stuffing (a little on the wetter side) and sprinkle on top. Bake uncovered at 350 for 1 hour or ½ hour if your meat has already been cooked. This is versatile in that you can swap out the chicken for a few cans of tuna. You can use turkey as well. Pork is another good substitute, using pork flavored stuffing.

SAUSAGE AND RICE CASSEROLE

Good for a side, a meal, or breakfast.

1 lb. sausage

3 cups cooked rice

1 can cream of mushroom soup

Crumble and fry sausage. Drain the fat. Combine sausage, rice, and mushroom soup and mix well. Bake at 350 for 30 minutes.

SHEPHERD'S PIE

I WAS RAISED on Shepherd's Pie made this way, so I always made it this way. It never occurred to me that there was any other way until the subject came up with my Idaho/Utah raised best friend. She said she didn't like Shepherd's Pie. Oh my! It's one of my favorites. When I told her how I make it. She made it and tried it this way—now she likes it. Apparently, in her neck of the woods, Shepherd's Pie is synonymous with kitchen sink.

This is another one of my go-to recipes for those times I forgot to take something out of the freezer for dinner...because I can brown the hamburger from frozen….and it's also a great go-to for using leftover mashed potatoes.

Preheat oven to 400 degrees
Serves 2, with leftovers

1 lb. hamburger
1 small onion
1 can whole kernel corn—drained well
3-4 cups mashed potatoes
Garlic powder

Chop onion finely and begin browning in a little oil. When onion is about ½ done, add in hamburger and garlic powder. Stir in salt and pepper. Season the hamburger well. While hamburger is cooking, spray bottom of 1 ½ quart baking dish with cooking spray. Place enough mashed potatoes to cover bottom. Then top with the corn.

Add the hamburger and onion mixture on top of the corn, when it's fully cooked. Smooth the remainder of the mashed potatoes over the top of the hamburger, covering the dish completely. Dot with butter and season with salt and pepper. Put in oven and bake until the top of the mashed potatoes is lightly browned. Serve like a casserole with bread.

MARYLAND CRAB CAKES

WILDLY POPULAR AND talked about all up and down the New England coast, on the menus of fine eateries everywhere… I had never had one, real or imitation, until it became one of the first new recipes I began cooking for myself when I became single. I'd always used the imitation crab the same two ways—in a salad and in scampi. It's fully cooked, making it quick food, but it's also a budget-friendly and healthy choice for my freezer. I'm not a fan of fish, but when they make it taste like something else, well, I'm there! Having never tasted real crab, they've got a customer in me. I'd also never had crab cakes before, so when I had these the first time four years ago, I was happy to now have three ways to enjoy the pollock the 'crab' is actually made of. So between the imitation crab company and this recipe, these Maryland Crab Cakes are a hit at sneaking fish into your diet!

1 pkg. imitation crab meat (about 1lb.)
¼ tsp. mustard
½ cup saltine crackers, crushed, plus some
1 tsp. old bay seasoning
Oil for frying tartar sauce (if preferred)
1 Tbsp. parsley
1 beaten egg, lg.

2 tsp. Worcestershire sauce

5 Tbsp. mayo

Combine crabmeat and all other ingredients. Then gently fold in cracker crumbs. Form six small rounded cakes or four larger, and then carefully dip in extra cracker crumbs on both sides and fry in small amount of oil. 1-2 minutes per side until golden brown. Drain on paper towels. Makes great leftovers reheated in the oven at 350 degrees for 15 minutes. Serve with tartar sauce.

BAKED CRAB RANGOON

MY BUDGET DOESN'T allow for eating out very often, but on the rare occasion when I can treat myself, Chinese takeout is my choice almost every time. I've had friends comment on how much more I eat when Chinese food is on the table. I admit, I can't help but stuff myself. Now that I can make a few dishes at home, I don't go quite as crazy as I used to....Do I, guys?

Time these just right and they'll be as crispy and crunchy as the ones from the Chinese restaurant—from *your* oven! So, they're not deep-fried and they're healthier! They taste exactly the same. Try some tonight with my MYO Lo Mein. Take out that you make in. You're going to love the taste and the savings—and you won't miss the fat one bit.

4 oz. imitation crab cut into small pieces

3 oz. cream cheese

⅛ tsp. garlic powder 1 small onion, finely chopped

⅛ tsp. salt 14 wonton wraps

⅛ tsp. Worcestershire sauce

Preheat oven to 425 degrees.

Mix first 5 ingredients together, and then gently fold in crab. Spoon mixture into center of wonton wrap. Wet edges with fingers dipped in water. Pull corners of wontons up to meet. Squeeze closed. Bake at 425 for 8-10 minutes or until golden brown and crispy. Makes 14.

TAMALE CASSEROLE

This casserole, like the others, is simple and inexpensive. It differs in that it's got a southwestern flair. When your budget says you can't go out for Mexican food, stay in and make this Tamale Casserole. You won't mind a bit. Preheat oven to 350F.

1 lb. hamburger
¼ lb. bulk pork sausage
1 small onion, chopped finely
1 clove garlic, chopped finely
1 ½ tsp. salt
1 ½ tsp. chili powder—more if you like
1 16 oz. can whole tomatoes with liquid
1 16 oz. can whole kernel corn, drained
1 can small pitted ripe olives, halved
1 cup yellow cornmeal
1 cup milk
2 eggs, well beaten
1 cup (4 oz.) shredded cheddar cheese

Cook hamburger, sausage, onion, and garlic until meats are browned, and drain off the fat. Stir in salt, chili powder, tomatoes, corn, and olives. Heat to boiling. Pour into 8x8 inch baking dish or 2 qt. round casserole dish.

Mix cornmeal, milk, and eggs and pour over the top of the meat mixture. Sprinkle with cheese and bake uncovered until golden brown, 40-50 minutes. Makes 6-8 Servings.

POTATOES

THESE CRISPY TREATS can be for breakfast as a hash brown or home fries substitute, can be a great dinner side, and can even be a vessel for a lunch dish. Lay a chicken tender or two across one of these. Mmm… Great lunch!

WAFFLED POTATOES

Cooking Spray
1 Potato, grated or shredded
½ yellow onion, grated
Cold water
2 Tbsp. oil
2 lg. eggs
½ tsp. salt and ¼ tsp. black pepper
(If you'd like yours spicy— ¼ tsp. cayenne pepper)

Wash your potato well and peel if you choose, but leaving the skin on is preferred. Shred or grate the potato then place the shreds in a bowl of cold water for 1-2 minutes. Remove with a slotted spoon to a clean towel and squeeze all of the water out.

Put shredded potato into clean bowl and grate ½ yellow onion. Mix with potato. Add in 2 Tbsp. oil, eggs, and salt & pepper. If using cayenne, add it now, too.

Heat waffle iron according to instructions that came with it, being sure to spray with cooking spray. Fill each waffle grid with enough potato mixture to

ALMOST cover, then close waffle iron. Mixture will spread out and fill.

Cook 5-8 minutes or until potatoes are golden brown and crispy. Top with usual toppings. Makes 2-3 waffled potatoes depending on the size of your potato and your waffle grids.

GARLIC ROASTED PARMESAN WEDGES

2 lg. potatoes
2 Tbsp. butter or Margarine
2 Tbsp. Parmesan Cheese
½ tsp. garlic powder
¼ tsp. salt
⅛ tsp. pepper

Heat oven to 425.

Wash potatoes and cut into wedges lengthwise. Put potatoes in pan and boil for 8-10 minutes, until just fork tender, then drain well. Microwave the butter until it's melted and pour into 9x13 baking pan. Stir in all other ingredients and add potatoes. Mix to coat with seasonings and bake for 10 minutes. Turn potatoes, and then bake another 10-15 minutes or until golden brown.

If you want these potatoes to be even fluffier, you can run them through a ricer while they're still warm. But just mashing or whipping will make them plenty good. A wonderful potato dish for a special occasion.

DELISH WHEN USED in my already good potato pancake recipe…. However, these potatoes are great as leftovers too, up to 3 days later. Just add a little milk before reheating.

PARMESAN MASHED POTATOES

3 lbs. (equals about 3-4 lg.) potatoes
S&P
¾ stick unsalted butter
¾ cup whole milk
¾ cup heavy cream
¾ cup parmesan cheese

Add last 5 ingredients to the cooked potatoes and mash or whip. Serve while still hot. An extra ½ cup whole milk can be substituted for the heavy cream, if desired.

POTATO PANCAKES

I came up with this recipe when I was first on my own because I couldn't seem to make a small enough amount of mashed potatoes for one person for one night. The next night, the leftovers would be there, and though I love mashed potatoes, frankly, eating them six nights a week was too much when I meant to have them only three.

I remembered potato pancakes from my childhood from a box mix. I LOVED those and recalled an onion flavor so I set out to try to recreate the potato pancakes I remember loving so much. This recipe exceeds that, crispy on the outside and fluffy on the inside, tons of flavor—I make extra mashed potatoes on purpose now.

These go well with any meat as a wonderful side, and if you fry them in bacon grease—yum! They're even good reheated the following day in a 400-degree oven on a greased cookie sheet.

2-3 cups mashed potatoes

2 eggs

1 lg. onion, grated by hand or chopped very fine in processor

½ tsp. garlic powder

½ tsp. salt

¼ tsp. black pepper

Flour

Oil for frying

Let your potatoes sit out to reach room temperature or heat slightly in microwave so that they are barely warm, but not hot. This will make them much easier to work with when mixing in seasonings and to shape into patties as well.

Once your potatoes have reached room temp, mix in the grated onion, garlic powder, and salt & pepper. Add the 2 eggs and stir very well.

At this point, add flour a little at a time stirring each time until your potato batter becomes stiff enough to shape into a ball.

Put 1-2 Tbsp. oil in a pan, and when it's very hot, put in a potato pancake that you have formed. Start by flouring your hands, pick up a good amount of the potato mixture, make a ball, and then flatten it to about ½ inch thick. Have some flour on a plate nearby that you can coat both sides of your pancake with before dropping it into the pan to fry. Fry quickly on both sides until golden brown and very crispy, then remove to drain on paper and salt them while hot.

Some people like to eat these with ketchup. My friends and I eat them salted just the way they are. So crispy on the outside and creamy yumminess inside. See what way will become your family's favorite.

PIZZA FLAVORED POTATOES

Potatoes
1 to 1 ½ cups mozzarella cheese
1 cup pepperoni finely chopped

Peel and thinly slice enough potatoes to fill a greased 6x9 casserole pan half way. Sprinkle cheese over potatoes and sprinkle pepperoni over that. You can also add mushrooms, olives or any other pizza topping you like.

Bake at 400 for 30 - 35 minutes or until potatoes are well cooked. Makes a great lunch or side dish.

AU GRATIN POTATOES

4 potatoes cut into slices (or two cups dehydrated potato slices)
½ onion sliced or onion flakes to taste
3 Tbsp. butter
3 Tbsp. flour
½ tsp. salt
1 ½ cups shredded cheddar cheese

Preheat oven to 400
Peel and slice potatoes or soak dehydrated potatoes until soft. In a small casserole pan, layer ½ the potatoes, then add onions and salt. Add the remaining potatoes. Melt butter, mix in flour and salt. Whisk for one minute. Stir in milk and cook until thickened. Stir in cheese and stir for one minute.

Pour mixture over potatoes. Bake for 1 ½ hours.

These potatoes are easy and a delicious change from baked or mashed. They reheat well, and you can add anything you may have leftover in your fridge to the filling —broccoli, hard-boiled eggs, squash, ham—so they become a wonderful way to use up leftovers. A great fall or winter dish, these will be a new favorite in your house. My kids loved them.

EASY TWICE BAKED POTATOES

1 baked potato per person
Butter
Milk
Minced onion (the dehydrated kind sold in the spice section)
Garlic powder
Salt and pepper
Parsley
¼ cup grated cheddar cheese per potato

Best to use Russet Potatoes, but others will work. Preheat oven to 425 F. Wash the potatoes well and prick with a fork. They will have the crispest skins and fluffiest insides if baked open—so put them on a cookie sheet if you wish, or directly onto oven racks. They will bake in about 45-50 minutes. Test with a fork.

Once your potatoes are cooked, remove from oven to cool. When they are cool enough to handle, cut them in half the long way and scoop the inside out of the skin, being careful to not tear the skins.

Set the skins aside and put all of the potato into a bowl. Add ½ tsp. butter and ½ tsp. milk for each whole potato (NOT EACH HALF), mix in ¼ tsp.

minced onion and garlic powder per potato as well. Salt and pepper to taste and add the cheddar cheese. Mash the potato mixture well. It will be lumpy, and that's ok. Now you can add any other things you may wish or leftovers you want to use. Just stir them in.

Put the potato skins in an 8x8 baking dish. Refill the skins with the mashed potato mixture, fill them well up over the tops of where you cut them, smooth the tops and round them over.

Sprinkle parsley and a little parmesan on top and put the refilled skins back into the oven until the tops are golden brown. About 4-6 minutes.

Be prepared to make these a lot.

THE CROCK-POT

HOMEMADE REFRIED BEANS

THESE ARE A great foundation for several dishes. It also makes a great side, served piping hot, sprinkled with cheese, onions, and sour cream. I make a large batch of refried beans, let cool, and then fill baggies. I freeze them until I need them for a recipe or side.

2 Tbsp. onion flakes or ½ onion finely chopped
2 cups dry pinto beans, rinsed
½ fresh jalapeno or other hot pepper, seeded and chopped
2 cloves garlic, minced
¾ teaspoons salt
½ tsp. black pepper
One big pinch of cumin
6 cups water
Combine all ingredients in slow cooker.
Cook on high for 8 hours.

Drain excess liquid, setting it aside. Mash remaining beans with a potato masher. As the beans become thicker, add back in some of the liquid until they are the right consistency. Store unused beans in freezer.

CROCK-POT APPLESAUCE

Peel and chop enough apples to fill the Crock-Pot.
Add 1 cup water
2 Tbsp. lemon juice
½ cup brown sugar
1 tsp. cinnamon
Optional: 1 tsp. pumpkin pie spice or ½ tsp. cloves and ½ tsp. nutmeg

Stir and cook on low for 6-8 hours. Stir and mash every half hour or so. Allow to cool and store in jars or bowls. This stores well in the fridge for about a week.

CROCK-POT STEWS

CROCK-POT STEWS ARE easy to create and customize. We eat stew at least twice a month, even through the summer.

The most basic stew is made with beef, potatoes, carrots, and any other veggie you'd like to add. Cut the meat up into small pieces. No worries if it's a cheap cut. A Crock-Pot will make the toughest meat tender. Add enough water to cover the meat and turn on high.

I add spices now. Season salt, garlic salt, onion and sometimes thyme or marjoram. Let cook for six hours until meat is tender. About 2 hours before you will serve, add the vegetables. I also add a packet of gravy and twice the water the gravy needs. Cover and let slow cook for another 2 hours or until the veggies are as tender as you'd like. Using the bread or French bread recipe, you can make bread bowls to serve this in. The same can be done with chicken. Just use chicken or poultry gravy.

SPAGHETTI

SINCE I DISCOVERED this, I make spaghetti in the Crock-Pot more often than not. This makes a big batch with plenty of leftovers.

Simply brown the hamburger, ground chicken, or turkey in a skillet. When it's cooked, add to the Crock-Pot. Over that, pour a jar of store bought or home canned spaghetti sauce, any additional spices you want to add, and one jar of water. Next, add a pound of spaghetti, broken into thirds. Over that, pour another jar of spaghetti sauce.

Cook on high for 3 hours or low for 6 hours. Stir once in a while after the noodles start to become soft enough.

I like to sprinkle parmesan and a bit of mozzarella cheese over the top a half hour before serving. Combined with Daisy's easy French bread, this is the perfect meal. (In this house, anyway.)

CHICKEN MAIN DISH

ONCE A MONTH, I will put a whole chicken in the Crock-Pot early in the morning. I sprinkle it with my go-to spices, garlic salt, season salt, pepper and onion, add about an inch of water, turn it on high and forget about it until dinner time.

This will literally fall apart when it's done, so plan on carving (or scooping) meat from the Crock-Pot onto plates or a serving dish. I'll do a basic side dish and veggie or salad.

I let the leftover chicken cool down and will debone either for another casserole type meal or for chopped lunchmeat through the week.

HAM, CHEESE, AND POTATO

HAS THERE EVER been a more beautiful food combination?

Use about two cups of diced ham, spices (seasoned salt, garlic, pepper and onion—can you tell I keep it simple even with spices? Feel free to play around with your own combinations)

Cut up 3-4 good sized potatoes and add those to the Crock-Pot. Add 1 cup of water and let cook on high for 3-4 hours. You can add shredded cheddar cheese right before serving or, using the mac and cheese white sauce recipe, pour that over the top about halfway through. I've had this turn out like a casserole and like a thick soup. Only the Crock-Pot God's know why. It's possible the different types of ham I've purchased had a different water content. Either way, the leftovers make a great lunch the next day.

PULLED PORK

AS OF THIS writing, pork is rather inexpensive. I'm actually buying more of that than ground beef and saving even more. Pork in the Crock-Pot can be cooked as a whole loin or roast, served with a side and veggie, or slow cooked all day and night in barbecue sauce and spices to make pulled pork for sandwiches.

TACO SOUP

TACO SOUP IS so popular these days. It seems like every restaurant is serving a taco soup. Here's one to make at home, frugally. Add a handful of nacho chips and a dollop of sour cream. Invite some friends over for this one—it's that good.

1 lb. ground beef

2 cans diced tomatoes

2 cans cooked beans of your choice. I like white beans.

1 can corn (optional)

1 pkg. taco seasoning (2-3 Tbsp. if you have a bulk pkg)

1 pkg. ranch dressing mix (optional)

8 oz. tomato sauce

1 chopped onion

2 cups water

1 tsp. cumin

Brown beef in skillet w/onion. Drain fat and add to Crock-Pot. Add all other ingredients (do not drain cans), and stir to mix. Cover and cook on low 8 hours or HIGH 4. I usually add more water and a little more taco seasoning powder to make it more like a soup.

SIDES

SIDE DISHES ARE pretty basic. They almost always consist of a potato, rice, bean, and pasta or bread variation.

BOSTON BAKED BEANS

2 cups navy beans
½ lb. bacon or ½ cup bacon bits
1 onion diced or ¼ cup onion flakes
3 Tbsp. molasses
2 tsp. salt
½ tsp. pepper
¼ tsp. dry mustard or 2 Tbsp. regular mustard
½ cup ketchup
1 Tbsp. Worcestershire
¼ cup brown sugar

Soak beans overnight. Simmer 1-2 hours then drain. Preheat oven to 325. Layer beans, bacon, and onion in casserole dish. In a saucepan, combine all other ingredients. Bring to a boil and pour over beans. Add enough water to cover the beans.

Bake for 3-4 hours.

VERSATILE RICE SIDE

I TWEAKED A recipe I found in order to make it more like the Rice-a-Roni side dish. It's one more thing I don't ever buy from the store now. It's extremely versatile so feel free to get creative and play around with the ingredients. By adding some leftover meat and veggies, you could create a rice casserole dinner. The list of what you can add to customize this is endless. Here's how I make it for a side dish.

1/4 cup spaghetti, vermicelli or angel hair pasta, broken into small pieces
1/2 cup uncooked rice (I use pearl or sushi rice)
3 cups water

2 Tbsp. butter
1 tsp. cornstarch
3 tsp. chicken bouillon
1/4 tsp. garlic powder
1/2 tsp. parsley
1/2 tsp. season salt
Pepper to taste

If I have time, I flash-cook the pasta. Melt the butter in a saucepan and add the broken pasta. Cook until browned and then add a half cup of the water. It will flash up, sizzle, and boil hard for a moment. Then add the rest of the water, rice, and spices. Cook over medium heat until rice is cooked and sauce is thickened. It's that easy.

If you wanted, you could use beef bouillon instead, and marjoram and thyme. You could use garlic salt, season salt, and taco seasoning for a Mexican side. You could use garlic salt, pepper, season salt, and a can of tuna for a quick meal. (Oh, throw in a few ounces of cream cheese at the end. That would be really tasty.) Heck, add peas to that, too. Use 2 tsp. of ham base, a leftover pork chop. No matter your spice/meat combination, be sure to add the cornstarch. This is just the base recipe for an endless number of combinations so experiment and have fun. It doesn't use a lot of expensive ingredients so you can afford to play around. This recipe as-is costs about twenty cents to make and will give four generous servings.

This can also be thrown together ahead of time in baggies and labeled. Then, you just add butter and water. You wouldn't be able to flash cook the pasta, but it's tasty either way.

EASY RICE AND BROCCOLI

RICE AND BROCCOLI go together like peas and carrots. This recipe puts them together in a quick side with flavor and easy preparation too. I say that makes it a winner. If you want, sprinkle some parmesan cheese on top.

Preheat oven to 375 F
2 cups hot water
1 pkg. (1- 1 ½ oz) onion soup mix
1 ⅓ cup instant rice
2 Tbsp. butter
1 tsp. salt
¼ tsp. pepper
1 Tbsp. lemon juice
1 (10 0z) pkg frozen broccoli either chopped or florets

Add hot water to onion soup mix, stir, and add rice, butter, salt, pepper and lemon juice. Put broccoli in greased 2 qt. ovenproof dish. Pour rice mix over broccoli. Cover with tight fitting lid or foil and bake in 375 F oven for 45 minutes. Makes 4 servings.

CORN FRITTERS

I'VE BEEN MAKING these for so long, I can't even remember how I came up with them or when. I do remember they were always one of my kids' favorite dinner sides, and a number of my friends over the years came to love them as well. I've cut the recipe down now. It used to make roughly 30 corn fritters. This recipe will make approximately 12, depending on what size you make. They're a great side for pork chops, ham, and chicken too. We eat them with a smear of butter, but I've had friends that eat them like pancakes with maple syrup! Find your bliss.

Now that it's just me, I don't make them often, but when I do, I freeze some. They still taste the same as they did all those years ago when my kids first enjoyed them—if I listened close, I bet I could hear my youngest asking for the butter to be passed.

2 cups dry pancake mix
Whether box or homemade, it doesn't matter.

What matters is the liquid.
*½ can **creamed** corn*

If you use a BOX mix, make pancake batter first, adding in only enough water to make batter thick. About 1 cup. Then add creamed corn.

If you use a homemade mix, omit the butter and use a little less than 1 cup of the milk, mix your batter, then add in creamed corn.

Once you have your batter ready, let it sit for 3-5 minutes while you heat your pan and oil it. Cook Daisy's Corn Fritters just like pancakes, making them approximately 3 inches across.

Keep them warm in the oven as you make more until finished. Oven set on 250. Serve piping hot.

BROCCOLI AND RICE SIDE

10-14 oz. frozen broccoli
1 cup cooked rice
2 cups shredded cheddar cheese

Cook broccoli—steam if possible. Cook the rice until soft. Mix together broccoli, rice, and shredded cheese. Pour into a small casserole dish and bake at 350 for 15 minutes.

PEAS AND CHEESE SIDE

2 cans peas (can also use 2 – 10 oz. packages of frozen)
1 cup shredded cheddar cheese
1 can cream of mushroom soup

Mix peas, cheese, and soup. Bake in a small, oiled casserole dish at 350 for 30 minutes.

EASY ONION RINGS

2 yellow onions, sliced
1 cup pancake mix
Water or milk. Enough to make a thick batter out of the pancake mix.

Mix pancake mix and just enough milk or water to make a heavy batter. Dip each onion ring to coat. Fry in a few inches of oil until golden brown. Drain on paper towels or a cloth. (I don't buy paper towels. I have one dishcloth that is dedicated to placing fried foods onto. Afterward, I use a lot of dish soap and let it soak. Then I wring it out and wash it.)

SUCCOTASH

WHEN I WAS a kid, I loved lima beans! I would eat an entire can of them. Now, I won't touch them. But, back then, Succotash was lima beans and creamed corn, at least here in the northeast. I've seen recipes for Succotash with many combinations of veggies, some that seem crazy to me. I guess it's about what you're used to, and how you were raised. So, I was raised in New England, and this is our version of Succotash.

2 cups whole kernel corn
2 cups cooked lima beans
3-4 Tbsp. half-and-half
½ tsp. salt
¼ tsp. black pepper
½ cup water

Combine corn and beans in medium-sized pan with ½ cup water. Bring to a boil, reduce heat to low and simmer for 10 minutes, allowing water to evaporate. Remove from heat. Add half-and-half and S&P toss and serve immediately.

CUCUMBER SALAD

A GREAT SUMMER veggie, the cucumber always seems destined to play a supporting role in salads and dishes. In this salad, the cucumber gets to be the star and we get to reap the benefits. Cool, low calorie, easy, inexpensive, and healthy—this salad may hang around your menu through the autumn.

2 medium cucumbers

1 small onion
1 ½ Tbsp. fresh dill
¼ tsp. salt
2-3 Tbsp. plain yogurt

Chop the cucumbers and onion small and place into a bowl. Drain off any liquid that accumulates. Add the dill, salt, and yogurt then stir. Chill well until serving time.

CORN WITH CREAM CHEESE

I LOVE VEGGIES, but as I see most things—veggies need pizzazz. Corn with real butter is yummy, add some salt and pepper, I'm there. But this corn... Now this corn has pizzazz.

¾ cup milk
1 3 oz. pkg cream cheese
1 Tbsp. butter
½ tsp. salt
⅛ tsp. pepper
2 cans whole kernel corn, drained well

Combine milk, cream cheese, butter, salt, and pepper in medium saucepan. Cook slowly over low heat stirring until cream cheese melts and all is blended well. Add drained corn and heat thoroughly. Makes 6 servings.

MAMA'S SWEET POTATOES

I CAN'T EVEN remember when I began making sweet potatoes this way or why. I just know it seems I always have. Even as an adult, my youngest son will only eat mine and made this way. When my kids gathered for Thanksgiving the first year after they'd all left home, all four asked if I made my sweet potatoes. Forget pies and turkey. My kids come home for Mama's sweet potatoes.

Sweet potatoes are pretty inexpensive at the harvest time of year in the fall, and canned ones are a pretty good substitute the rest of the time. They pack a lot of nutrition, tons of flavor, and are cost effective, ounce per ounce. And hey, if they bring your children home, that's quite a bonus.

Serves 6
5-6 Fresh Yams or Sweet Potatoes
2 Tbsp. Butter
Splash of Milk
1-2 Tbsp. Maple Syrup
Pinch of Cinnamon
Dash of Nutmeg— (little more than the cinnamon)
2-3 Tbsp. Brown sugar
Salt

Peel and wash the potatoes, then cut into pieces. About 6 pieces should work. Boil the potatoes until they are done well. Drain. Put potatoes in a bowl and mash like regular potatoes with the butter and milk. Don't worry about getting them creamy yet. Add in the brown sugar, maple syrup, nutmeg, and cinnamon. Now beat with a fork. If they're not creamy and fluffy, add a little more milk. Be careful not to add too much. Taste and see if the sweetness is to your taste. You may want more brown sugar. Also, some potatoes are sweeter than others are so you may need more for that reason. When they're the way you want, smooth the top like you're frosting a cake… and salt the top of the potatoes. The combination of salty and sweet in this dish is what makes it amazingly yummy! Serve with butter on each portion.

CARROT FRITTERS

THESE FRITTERS ARE vegetarian, but not vegan as they contain butter or bacon drippings.

A great way to sneak some vegetables into your diet, this recipe shows carrots in a whole new light. Serve them with honey or maple syrup, accompanied by some fried ham, and you're sure to never need glasses.

1 ½ cups grated raw carrot

3 Tbsp. grated onion

3 cups bread crumbs

¾ tsp. baking powder

2 lg. eggs, beaten

¼ cup milk

½ tsp. salt

⅛ tsp. pepper

3 Tbsp. bacon drippings or butter

Combine all ingredients except bacon drippings or butter. Mix well. Form patties about 3 inches in diameter, you will get 12. Heat butter or bacon drippings in frying pan, place patties in pan when it's hot. Brown on both sides. Makes 6 servings of 2 fritters each.

SNACKS

TACO CHIP DIP

8 oz. container sour cream
1 package (8oz) cream cheese softened
1 package taco seasoning (1 ½ oz. if using bulk or homemade)

Mix all ingredients together and beat until smooth. Refrigerate for a few hours before using. This is great with corn chips as well as on top of dinners like loaded burritos or enchiladas.

VEGETABLE DIP

1 cup cottage cheese
1 cup mayonnaise
1 package ranch dressing mix

Optional: stir in dried onions or chopped green onions. Mix all ingredients well. Refrigerate until ready to place on a vegetable tray.

TUNA BALL

Great with crackers.
8 oz. cream cheese softened

½ a package of dry onion soup mix
1 (6oz) can of tuna in water, drained.

Mix all ingredients until smooth. Form into ball and refrigerate 6 hours before serving.

SAUSAGE BALLS

I GREW UP with these. My grandmother made them all the time and while I still can't make them just like she did, I still enjoy them.

2 cups bulk biscuit mix
1 lb. sausage
1 cup shredded cheddar cheese—In all honesty, I use 2-3 cups. But not everyone is a cheese freak like me.

Mix all ingredients, using hands if needed. Form into balls. Place in a pan. I use jellyroll pan or cast iron skillet to catch the grease. Bake at 350 for 20 minutes. Great to make ahead and warm up with eggs and toast for breakfast!

POPCORN IS CONSIDERED a staple around here and I had no idea how many different ways you could make it until I saw Pauline's book, Pop'n Corn. She has over 100 recipes for popcorn. It's also available on Amazon.

CRISPY HOT WINGS

IF I WERE told to pick one food that I had to eat for all eternity, hot wings would be it. I love them, but they have to be right. They cannot be dry, so crispy that the meat adheres to the bone, or too mild. The perfect combination of moist enough, crisp enough, and spicy enough is my idea of wing heaven.

10-15 uncooked chicken wings
2 eggs
2 Tbsp. hot sauce of your choice
2 Tbsp. crushed red pepper
1 Tbsp. black pepper
1 Tbsp. cayenne pepper
Flour
Pan of oil or deep fryer for frying

Combine the eggs, hot sauce, and seasonings in a medium-sized bowl and beat until foamy. Pour flour into another medium sized bowl. Dip each wing in the flour coating it well, and then set aside. Once all of the wings are coated with flour, dip them in the egg mixture, then back into the flour bowl *again* and set on a plate to dry. 5-8 minutes. Fry at 350 for 8-10 minutes or until they float to the surface.

APPLESAUCE COOKIES

¾ cup butter
½ cup applesauce
2 ¼ cup flour
1 cup brown sugar
¾ tsp. cinnamon

½ cup walnuts

1 egg

1 cup raisins

1 tsp. baking soda

Pinch of salt

¼ tsp. ground cloves

Mix butter, egg, and sugar well then stir in applesauce and add dry ingredients. Mix in nuts and raisins. Drop by teaspoons onto cookie sheet. Bake at 375 for 10-12 minutes. Store in tightly closed container or jar.

CHOCOLATE CHIP COOKIES

¾ cup sugar

¾ cup brown sugar

1 cup butter

1 egg1 tsp. baking soda

2 ¼ cups flour

½ tsp. salt

1 package chocolate chips

Mix sugar, brown sugar, butter and egg until creamy. Add baking soda, salt and flour and mix well. Add chocolate chips last. Bake at 350 for ten to twelve minutes.

The secret to gooey chocolate chip cookies is to watch them carefully and **take them out when they look like they could use two more minute**s. Then smack the cookie pan on the stove or counter and they will collapse into soft, gooey goodness. This works for every cookie variety I've ever tried it on.

GRANOLA BARS

This is a fantastic replacement for store bought bars both in taste and in fiber content.

2 ½ cups rice cereal

2 cups oats (I use steel cut)

½ cup raisins

½ cup brown sugar

½ cup corn syrup

½ cup peanut butter

1 tsp. vanilla

½ cup chocolate chips

Combine cereal, oats, and chocolate chips in a large bowl. Bring brown sugar and corn syrup to a boil, stirring constantly. Remove from heat. Add peanut butter and vanilla. Pour over cereal and oats and stir until coated. Press into 9x13 pan and allow to cool. Cut into bars.

MUG CAKE!

THIS IS THE perfect quick snack or dessert for one. It's also handy to measure dry ingredients into a baggie with written instructions so kids can make a quick snack in the microwave.

3 Tbsp. flour
2 Tbsp. sugar
1 ½ Tbsp. cocoa powder
¼ tsp. baking powder
Pinch of salt.
3 Tbsp. milk
1 ½ Tbsp. oil
1 Tbsp. peanut butter

Mix the dry ingredients in a coffee mug. Add the wet ingredients and stir. Microwave for 1 minute 10 seconds. Times might vary slightly with different microwaves.

FROSTING:

1/4 cup powdered sugar
1 Tbsp. baking cocoa (optional)

148

1 Tbsp. butter
1/4 tsp. vanilla
Milk

Mix sugar, cocoa and vanilla. Add just enough milk to create a frosting consistency. Omit cocoa for vanilla frosting, replace with peanut butter for peanut butter frosting.

DESSERTS

STANDARD PIECRUST

IT'S NOT THAT hard to get the hang of making piecrust. If at first you don't succeed in rolling it out in a circle, using the pat in pan method is fine. And if you can, use lard. It really does result in a tastier, flakier crust.

Two crust - Ten-inch pie
1 cup shortening or lard
2 ⅔ cup flour
1 tsp. salt
7-8 Tbsp. cold water

Blend the flour, salt, and shortening until the mixture resembles coarse crumbs. Stir in water a Tbsp. at a time until mixture forms a ball. Split into two balls. Roll each out to fit a 10-inch pie plate. Place crust in pie plate. Press the dough evenly into the bottom and sides of two pie plates.

SINGLE CRUST — TEN-INCH PIE

½ cup shortening
1 ⅓ cup flour
½ tsp. salt
3-4 Tbsp. water

Use the same directions as for the double crust.

GRAHAM CRACKER CRUST

1 ½ cups crushed graham crackers
⅓ cup butter, melted
3 Tbsp. sugar

Add the sugar and butter to the crushed graham crackers. Mix well until all crumbs are wet. Press into a pie pan.

COOKIE CRUST

1 ½ cup crushed vanilla wafers
¼ cup butter melted.

Blend crushed wafers and butter together. Press into pan. (This is wonderful for banana cream pie.)

CHOCOLATE PUDDING

SOME RECIPES JUST make me happy. This is one of them. It's one of my favorite from scratch comfort foods. I eat it cold in the summer and hot in the winter. While this recipe takes a bit of unsweetened cocoa, it's well worth it. Did I mention it's really easy?

CHOCOLATE PUDDING

1 1/2 cups sugar
1 cup unsweetened cocoa
6 Tbsp. cornstarch
6 cups of milk

Mix everything together in a large saucepan over medium to med-high heat. It will look like it doesn't want to come together but it will as it warms up. Whisk often scraping the bottom as it slowly heats and thickens. Boil for one minute. Either pour into a large bowl or into individual serving dishes.

This is a large batch. Feel free to cut it in half or thirds. I make a lot because we will have it for dessert, and then I'll put the leftovers in half pint jars for portable snacks the next day. (You can also use small Gladware containers.) This completely replaces the need for pudding cups.

And, because I like to shave minutes where I can, while this was slowly heating, I made up four baggies ready to go for next time.

NO CHURN PEANUT BUTTER ICE CREAM

8 oz. cream cheese softened to room temperature
1 cup peanut butter
1 ½ cups powdered sugar
1 ½ cups milk
16 oz. cool whip (thawed)

Blend cream cheese and peanut butter in a mixer until smooth. Add powdered sugar and milk. Beat until smooth. Stir in cool whip and mix by hand until blended. Pour into dish or bowl and place in the freezer overnight. This is absolutely divine when topped with homemade Magic Shell topping, but also wonderfully rich alone.

SHORTBREAD COOKIES

2 cups flour
½ cup brown sugar
½ lb. butter (softened to room temperature. No margarine.)

Mix flour and sugar. Cut in butter until crumbly. The lumps should be reduced to no bigger than pea-sized. Pat into the bottom of a casserole pan or a jelly roll pan. Bake at 325 for 40 minutes. Cut into squares and let cool. You can also make into one-inch balls and press down as you would peanut butter cookies. Eat plain or dust with powdered sugar, jam, or jelly.

LEMON BARS

A CLASSIC RECIPE that never gets boring, doesn't require a lot of ingredients, and is loved by young and old. A great dessert for every season, all occasions, and anytime. The perfect picnic dessert. The crust is so meltingly tender, it disappears when it touches your tongue, leaving you with a sweetness that just complements the lemon curd perfectly. I made these the other evening, shared 3... and I'm not ashamed to say, ate all of the rest since.

CRUST:

1 ⅓ cups flour
¼ cup sugar
½ cup softened butter or margarine

FILLING:

¾ cup sugar
2 eggs
2 Tbsp. flour
¼ tsp. baking powder
3 Tbsp. Lemon Juice
Powdered Sugar

Preheat oven to 350 degrees. In a small bowl, combine all crust ingredients and mix until crumbly—2-3 minutes. Press this mixture into the bottom of an 8x8" square pan and bake for 15-20 minutes or until edges are lightly browned. While the crust is baking, combine filling ingredients in another small bowl and beat at low speed until well mixed. Pour the filling over hot crust when it comes out of the oven, then return to oven and bake for another 18-20 minutes or until filling is set. Sprinkle with powdered sugar and cool. Cut into bars when cooled, and serve.

QUICK, FRIED FRUIT PIES

LIKE MY CO-AUTHOR, I don't always make everything from scratch, especially if I find a bargain on something that I can use many ways. Two ingredients in this recipe, "pop biscuits" and fruit pie fillings, are exactly what I mean. Both are very versatile, and often I can find good sales on them at holiday time. Pop biscuits can be used many ways, for every meal, and a whole world of desserts, while pie fillings have endless uses as well. For this recipe, we'll put them together, and make a wonderful fried pie that's fast and easy—and the best part? They cost pennies to make. Buy your items on sale, and they're even cheaper. For those of you who can your own fruits, this'll be a steal.

1 can buttermilk 'pop' biscuits
1 can fruit pie filling of your choice
1 cup powdered sugar
3 tsp. cinnamon
2 Tbsp. oil

Roll out the biscuits until they are the size of a small saucer sized plate. Spoon a tablespoonful of pie filling into the center of each flattened biscuit and fold over in half. Tuck in edges and crimp with a fork. Repeat until they are all done. Bring oil to med. heat. Fry pies on both sides to golden brown crispness. Make a mixture of powdered sugar, cinnamon and water until consistency of glaze and drizzle over pies before they cool.

TASTY FRY BREAD (SCONES)

Using inexpensive pop biscuits, roll out each biscuit flat. Drop in oil heated to 375. Without a thermometer, a good way to test the oil is to pinch off a small piece of dough and drop it in. If it begins to sizzle and bobs to the top, you should be fine. Too low an oil temperature will cause the food to absorb too much oil. Too high a temp and the outside will cook quickly while the center remains raw. Cook on each side for a few minutes until each side is golden brown. Remove and place on a paper towel or hand towel to cool. Top with a sprinkle of confectioners' sugar, jelly, jam, honey butter, or frosting.

BREAD PUDDING

Preheat oven to 350
Makes 9x13 inch pan
6 Slices day old bread
2 Tbsp. melted butter
½ cup raisins
4 beaten eggs
2 cups milk
¾ cup sugar
1 tsp. vanilla
1 tsp. cinnamon

Break bread into small pieces into 9x13 inch pan, drizzle melted butter over it, and sprinkle with raisins. In medium-sized bowl, combine eggs, milk, sugar, cinnamon and vanilla—beat until well mixed and pour over bread. Lightly push down with fork. Bake 45 minutes or until top springs back.

RICE PUDDING

THIS RECIPE IS the *BEST* for using up leftover white rice! Another of those classics, like lemon bars, never stops being a favorite.

>   *1 cup uncooked white rice*
>   *2 cups water*
>   *3 beaten eggs*
>   *2 cups milk*
>   *½ cup sugar*
>   *1 tsp. vanilla*
>   *½ tsp. salt*
>   *⅓ cup raisins*
>   *¼ tsp. nutmeg*

Boil rice 25-30 minutes. Allow to cool. Preheat oven to 325. In a large bowl, combine—eggs, milk, sugar, vanilla, and salt. Stir in cooked rice and raisins and mix well then pour into 8x8 baking dish. Bake uncovered 30 minutes, stir, then sprinkle nutmeg on top and bake another 30 minutes or until knife inserted in center comes out clean.

HAWAIIAN CRISP

THIS RECIPE IS great for using up bananas that you have around that may be just on the edge of getting too ripe for eating by themselves, but cooked up in this dessert with a few other odds and ends, they won't be wasted and will be a dessert everyone will love. Feel free to substitute whatever you have on hand and make this something new that you and yours will love.

Preheat oven to 350
1 lg. can pineapple chunks drained
or a fresh pineapple peeled and cubed
4 medium bananas sliced
¼ cup brown sugar
2 Tbsp. Flour

TOPPING:

⅓ cup old fashioned oats
¼ cup flour
2 Tbsp. shredded coconut, toasted. (To toast: spread on cookie sheet, bake at 350 for 5-10 minutes stirring frequently)
2 Tbsp. brown sugar
¼ tsp. nutmeg
¼ cup chilled butter, cut into cubes
Cooking spray

In a large bowl, combine pineapple and bananas, sprinkle with brown sugar and flour, and toss to coat evenly. Spray 11x7-inch pan and pour pineapple and bananas into it. In another bowl, mix first 5 TOPPING ingredients, cut in butter until mixture is crumbly, and sprinkle over pineapple mixture.

Bake 30-35 minutes or until filling is bubbly and topping is golden brown.

Serve warm or at room temperature.

Extra wonderful with a scoop of vanilla ice cream!

ANOTHER QUICK AND easy way to use up those leftover bananas is this pudding recipe. Pudding is a great choice because it's quick and a good summertime dessert. Though your bananas can be used in the Hawaiian Crisp or Molly's Banana Bread recipe—great when you may want to turn the oven on—this pudding will use them up on hot days when you don't. Easy, fast, made with things you may already have in your pantry, I guarantee there will be no leftovers. Now that's frugal.

BANANA PUDDING

2 pkg. (3 ½ oz) ea. Instant vanilla pudding
1 can (14 oz) sweetened condensed milk (NOT EVAPORATED*)
1 (8 oz) container Non-dairy whipped topping
6 large ripe bananas
1 (11oz) box vanilla wafers

Prepare the pudding according to the directions on the box. Let it chill until slightly thickened. About 5 minutes. Mix in the condensed milk and the non-dairy topping. Slice the bananas into ½ inch slices. Layer the vanilla wafers, bananas, and nondairy topping mixture in a clear glass bowl or 9x13x2 inch glass pan alternating layers. Serve immediately or refrigerate and serve later.

*See Molly's Make Your Own Sweetened Condensed Milk Recipe in this book if you want to make it yourself.

PEANUT BUTTER FUDGE

½ C = 1 Stick butter

2 ¼ cup brown sugar
½ cup milk
¾ cup peanut butter
1 tsp. vanilla
3 ½ cup confectioners' sugar

Melt butter in a pan on low and stir in brown sugar and milk. Bring to a boil for 2 minutes stirring frequently. Remove from heat, stir in peanut butter and vanilla, and pour over confectioners' sugar in a large bowl. Beat until smooth. Pour into 8x8 pan. Chill until firm, in fridge. Cut into squares and serve.

NO BAKE COOKIES

2 cups sugar
¼ cup cocoa
½ cup milk
½ cup butter
1 tsp. vanilla
½ cup peanut butter
3 cups oatmeal

Combine sugar, cocoa, milk, and butter. Bring to a boil. Boil for one minute then stir in vanilla, peanut butter, and oats. Spoon onto waxed paper or greased cookie sheet. Allow to cool.

MOCK PECAN PIE

Every well-stocked pantry has oatmeal in it, the main ingredient in this 'no pecan' pecan pie. In these hard times, we get a meal on the table, and we're grateful for that. Desserts and snacks are the first things we pare from our budgets and menus. It's wonderful to have recipes like this so that even though we may not have all the bells and whistles, we can still enjoy a good old-fashioned dessert and not break the bank. This recipe is frugal and fast.

Preheat oven to 350 F
1 unbaked pie shell, 9-inch
¼ cup butter or margarine
½ cup sugar
½ tsp. cinnamon
½ tsp. ground cloves
¼ tsp. salt
1 cup dark corn syrup
3 lg. eggs
1 cup quick oats

Cream together butter and sugar, add cinnamon and cloves, stir in salt, and then mix in syrup. Add eggs one at a time, stirring after each, until blended well, then stir in oats. Pour into piecrust and bake at 350F for about an hour or until knife inserted in center comes out clean.

POUND CAKE

THIS DESSERT IS simple but versatile. It can be eaten plain or topped with berries, ice cream, whipped cream, just about anything. It's best a day or two after it's made and can be made from items everyone has on hand at any given time. Pound cake has always been one of my favorites, Lemon especially. Use Molly's recipe for evaporated milk to make this even more inexpensive.

Preheat oven to 350F
2 ¼ cups sugar
1 ¼ cups butter or margarine
1 tsp. vanilla
5 lg. eggs
3 cups flour
1 tsp. baking powder
¼ tsp. salt
1 cup evaporated milk
Grease and flour 10 x 4-inch loaf pan.

Beat sugar, vanilla, butter, and eggs in large bowl on low speed, scraping bowl well, for 1 min. Beat on high speed, continuing to remember to scrape the bowl well, for 5 minutes. Now, beat in flour, baking powder and salt, alternating with milk on low speed until all are added. Pour into pan. Bake until toothpick inserted in center comes out clean. About 70-80 minutes. Cool 20 minutes then remove from pan. If you want to make lemon flavor, substitute lemon extract for vanilla and fold 2-3 tsp. lemon zest into batter.

SHOOFLY PIE

THIS PIE IS just about the epitome of frugal. It uses a single crust, molasses, a few simple pantry items, and some spices. With those few things adding up to *pie,* I'm already at the table.

Preheat oven to 400F
Prepare pastry for 9-inch one-crust pie
Filling:
¾ cup flour
½ cup brown sugar
3 Tbsp. butter
½ tsp. salt
½ tsp. cinnamon
¼ tsp. ground ginger
⅛ tsp. nutmeg
¾ cup hot water
½ tsp. baking soda
½ cup dark molasses
1 egg yolk, well beaten

Mix flour, brown sugar, butter, and spices with hands until crumbly. In another bowl mix water and baking soda, then add in molasses and egg yolk and stir well. Pour the molasses mixture into prepared piecrust, then sprinkle the brown sugar mixture over the top of it. Bake 15 minutes then reduce the oven temp to 325F and bake until crust and topping are browned, about 20 minutes or so. Serve warm.

I LOVE COOKIES! Everyone that knows me, knows I love cookies. I am crazy about chocolate cookies, chocolate everything really; but when it comes to homemade cookies—these have my heart.

GINGER SNAPS

DO NOT PREHEAT oven. You will need to refrigerate your cookie dough for 2 hours before rolling and baking.

1 cup sugar
½ cup shortening
1 cup dark molasses
½ cup water
4 cups flour
1 ½ tsp. salt
1 ½ tsp. ground ginger
1 tsp. baking soda
1 /2 tsp. ground cloves
½ tsp. nutmeg
½ tsp. allspice
Sugar for tops

Mix 1 cup sugar, shortening, molasses, and water in large bowl. Stir in all remaining ingredients except sugar for tops. Cover and refrigerate for at least 2 hours.

Preheat oven to 375F. Roll dough on WELL-floured surface, to ¼ inch thick. Cut into 3-inch circles with large cookie cutter or large sized jar. Place about 1-1 ½ inches apart on ungreased cookie sheet and bake until no mark remains when touched. 10-12 minutes is usual. Cool 2 minutes then remove from cookie sheet. Makes about 2 ½ dozen.

HOLIDAY TIPS

Feasting Frugal

Daisy

HOLIDAYS WERE ALWAYS a big deal in our house when my kids were growing up. Decorations galore, gifts, and food...lots of yummy food. For the holidays I, like most people, made foods I didn't make the rest of the year. I started baking two to three weeks prior and froze much of it in order to have everything done in time and made everything in triplicate.

My kids would talk about it and daydream about it for that entire time. Pies, breads, cookies, cookie bars, muffins, and the grand meal itself. I usually made 6-8 pies, and every year, I tried to change a few out, of course keep the favorites, but add some new ones.

At some point, I'd added cheesecake too, and one year, when my youngest son John was just into his teenage years, I added ice cream pie. I'd never made it, had no recipe, just decided I was going to make this ice cream pie, and had an idea how to go about it. The first year it was a huge success and a big hit with everyone. I made it last thing, the night before the holiday, once all of the other desserts were done. Exhausted, and looking at a kitchen full of dirty dishes, I was done.

So, the following year, I decided to do exactly the same thing. On the eve of the holiday, my son John was helping me do a few things, I was worn out, and about to be finished with the cheesecake, and call it a night after washing a few dishes. Then John asked me when we were making the ice cream pies.

I was floored. I'd forgotten.

Not one to leave anything undone, I told him we were doing them "right now." This was at about 10pm.

Now, to make ice cream pie, you need *softened* ice cream….

This is where this story goes wrong…but makes for a great memory.

Because it was so late, I was tired and had a full day of cooking and company ahead of me early in the morning—I wanted to do these ice cream pies and be done. I had John pull the ice cream out of the deep freeze while I got the cookie crusts prepared.

We worked together on those, and when they were done, which only took about fifteen minutes, I turned my attention to the ice cream, which would be the filling. It was still pretty frozen. I made the executive decision to go ahead with the project anyway. I was tired, remember?

Putting the ice cream in a bowl, and covering it with some chocolate syrup, I was feeling reasonably sure that my electric mixer would muddle through and whip this frosty cube into pie goodness. John asked if he could do the whipping. I gave him the go-ahead while I headed to the sink to wash more of the endless dishes.

As I turned my back, I heard the mixer start and then struggle as John sank it into the chocolate arctic. He said nothing, the mixer groaned on, and I washed my dishes.

Momentarily, I heard that word all females with children know so well, "Mom…...!"

As I turned, I caught the scent before John could say more or before I could ask what was wrong. Then, the mixer quieted and quit. Walking closer to where he stood with the now-dead mixer in his hand, I was aware of the smell of burnt something. We both looked at each other in surprise, like we hadn't expected THAT… so quiet... like…. jeez…. We didn't know that was going to happen. Now what are we going to do? Then we laughed and made jokes about killing the mixer. For a minute, I wasn't sure what to do. Then, after laughing about it for a while, I wasn't tired anymore and kicked into gear. I FINALLY let the ice cream soften (DUH) and mixed it by hand, and the pies came out just fine that way.

It sure made for a funny holiday story, how John and I killed the mixer. And how we killed it trying to whip *frozen* ice cream, no less.

Just last year, John and I remembered that story again and laughed about it when he was about to use my new mixer... for POTATOES... cooked ones.

THIS RECIPE IS meant to be quick and easy—and it's pretty inexpensive. You're getting two pies for about $7 if you make your own chocolate syrup. That's $3.50 a pie. Pretty cheap for pie with store bought goods.

It will take about 25-30 minutes total to make it the way I make it. Great for a fast dessert you need to have last minute. And remember to take the ice cream out at least 30 minutes ahead. Covered well, this will last in the freezer for at least 2-3 months.

CHOCOLATE ICE CREAM PIE

Makes 2
1 roll of chocolate chip cookie dough
(Or you can make your own)
1 lg. size bowl of nondairy topping
1 half gal choc ice cream
Chocolate Syrup—Use Molly's MYO chocolate syrup recipe!
Any other ice cream toppings you like—sprinkles, etc.

Open cookie dough and press small amounts at a time into bottoms of pie pans and up sides to form crust for pies. Bake in oven according to directions, making sure not to overbake. It will stick together and stay in one piece if you do this quickly while dough is still cool/cold. If it gets too warm, refrigerate it for a bit, then finish. While the cookie crusts are baking, work on the ice cream fillings.

Put SOFTENED ice cream in a large bowl and whip. Add about ½ cup chocolate syrup and mix in. Add in nuts or sprinkles, anything else you may want, about ¼ cup. Don't let your ice cream melt while waiting for the cookie crusts. If it gets too soft, put it in the freezer for a minute.

When the cookie crusts are done, put them in the freezer for a couple of minutes to cool quickly. When cooled, pour half of the ice cream mixture into each pie pan. Smooth the top over and put half of the nondairy topping on each pie. Smooth it out. Drizzle with chocolate syrup and put into freezer immediately. Pies will be ready to serve in 15 minutes.

Molly

I DON'T HAVE specific recipes for holiday meals because there are already thousands out there. But I'll share with you how I tackle the most expensive meals of the year.

It's hard not to fall for all the marketing at Christmastime and food marketing is no exception. They say that the average cost for Christmas dinner is fifty dollars. I know for a fact it can be at least double, if not triple that. The ingredients alone for Chex Mix are nearly thirty dollars. (And Chex mix is a *must have* in this house during the holidays.)

It boggles my mind how many people are out buying all of a holiday dinner on the eve of that holiday.

I keep costs down by gathering up things I'll need well in advance. Months in advance. I'll start buying the Chex cereal during the back to school sales. I get the mixed nuts early too before the holidays push the price up. I make sure there are a few extra pounds of butter tucked away in the freezer. I like to have a meat, cheese, and cracker tray so I'll need to at least buy the crackers ahead of time. I'll buy summer sausage in October and freeze it. As a rule, I plan the Thanksgiving and Christmas menu months in advance. By breaking my list down to ingredients, I can spot sales well before the holiday.

There are rarely sales on turkeys outside this quarter of the year, so I wait for that mega sale early in November. In my neck of the woods, you can get a turkey for a third of the price if you spend X amount of dollars in one trip. So I'll buy it on a regular shopping trip sometime in early November. (One year I missed the sale so we had ham.) Another option is to buy a turkey breast. This works well for 2-4 people. With only a few people, I'd even consider using a whole chicken. Again, it's the *marketing* that tells us we MUST have a massive turkey on our table on *this night* of the year. I don't buy it and I'm not afraid to get creative.

My Thanksgiving and Christmas menus are usually identical. Only it's turkey (or some form of poultry) in November and it's ham in December that changes.

On the holiday, I make biscuits and gravy or cinnamon rolls for breakfast. The rest of the day we graze. About eleven, I will put out Chex mix, fruit salad, a meat-cheese-cracker tray, vegetable tray, and egg nog.

Dinner is the main meat, mashed potatoes and gravy, dinner rolls (or bread), stuffing, cranberry sauce, mac and cheese, sweet potatoes, southern style green beans (or French onion green beans) and deviled eggs.

I make each of these dishes in **much** smaller quantities than I normally make. First, we've already been grazing all day so no one is starving. Second, with so many side dishes, I don't need to make as much. I use several one-quart glass dishes. There are usually enough leftovers for lunch the next day plus snacking over the weekend and very little goes to waste.

Everything is made from scratch except for the eggnog, cranberry sauce, and stuffing. For the life of me, I can't seem to get the hang of homemade stuffing. So I'll spend a buck on that. (Literally, a buck. I won't buy it until it's on sale.)

Dessert is always pumpkin and apple pie. (And some fudge if the kids talk me into it.)

Besides defining a menu and a shopping list well in advance, consider having a "Do Not Touch" box in your pantry. Store things you'd like to reserve for holidays there. (Leftover clearance candy from Halloween applies here if you can use it for holiday treats.) I already have stuffing, cranberry sauce, walnuts, and some pecans in mine. If I leave them in with the rest of the pantry goods, chances are they will be used up.

When you start preparing months ahead of time, you should be able to whip out holiday meals without feeling it in the wallet at all.

DRINKS

LAST YEAR, I went on a tear trying to recreate as much store bought food as I could. One that had me stumped for a while was chocolate syrup. If you have small children (or a large sweet tooth), chances are this is a staple in your house. Here is a scratch recipe for chocolate syrup that tastes so close to the real thing, my kids couldn't tell the difference. It's perfect for chocolate milk and as an ice cream topper, too. Best of all, it cost pennies to make.

CHOCOLATE SYRUP HACK

Mix together in a saucepan:
2 cups sugar
1 cup water
1/2 cup unsweetened cocoa
1 tsp. vanilla

Stir constantly over medium heat until boiling then boil for 3 minutes. That's it! Pour into a pint jar or heat resistant jar and store in the fridge up to ten days. Ours never lasts ten days and it never makes it to the fridge before the boys make a glass of chocolate milk.

If after ten days, it starts to crystallize, simply reheat until the sugar dissolves and use right away.

HOT COCOA

CAN'T HAVE TOO much. Honestly, a 55-gallon barrel might work. I make my own and have a few months' worth on hand at the start of autumn. Here's the recipe I use:

12 cups instant milk
3 cups coffee creamer
4 cups sugar
2 ½ cups cocoa

Mix and store. (Gotta love simplicity.)

To use, add 3 TBSP (or so) per cup of milk in a saucepan and heat on medium until blended and smooth. This is not instant. Good things come to those who wait. Pour into mugs and top with marshmallows.

MOCHA ESPRESSO COFFEE MIX

½ cup instant coffee granules

½ cup sugar

2 cups powdered milk

½ cup coffee creamer powder (store brand works fine)

¼ cup cocoa

¼ cup chocolate pudding mix

Blend all ingredients well. Store in an airtight container. Use ¼ cup of mix per 8 oz. hot water.

RICH VANILLA COFFEE MIX

⅓ cup instant coffee granules

1 cup powdered milk

½ cup coffee creamer powder

⅓ cup sugar

¼ cup vanilla pudding mix

Blend all ingredients well. Store in an airtight container. Use ¼ cup of mix per 8 oz. hot water.

TOFFEE COFFEE MIX

½ cup instant coffee granules
1 cup powdered milk
½ cup coffee creamer powder
½ cup brown sugar
¼ cup butterscotch pudding mix

Blend all ingredients well. Store in an airtight container. Use ¼ cup of mix per 8 oz. hot water.

HOMEMADE ELECTROLYTE SPORTS DRINK

ALL SPORTS DRINKS do is to replace the salt while sweating and the glucose used by muscles during hard work. That they are weakly flavored make it more palatable.

2 qts. water
5 - 10 Tbsp. sugar
1 tsp. salt (pink Himalayan is the best but table salt will do. You could also use a salt/potassium blend.)
1 package unsweetened Kool-Aid, any flavor.

Mix everything together and chill. Adjust the sugar to your own taste. You could also use honey with a lemon flavor Kool-Aid packet. This recipe has saved quite a bit of money over the hot summers here where my kids used to drink a lot of sports drinks.

MYO (MAKE YOUR OWN)

COFFEE CREAMER

I LITERALLY DANCED when I figured out how to make chocolate caramel coffee creamer. Then I went on a creation spree and came up with several other varieties. My husband loves the chocolate hazelnut. No more store-bought coffee creamer here! This is just as good at a fraction of the cost. If you make the corn syrup and evaporated milk, it's so frugal it's crazy. Here are two basic recipes you can tweak to your own personal like.

VANILLA SPICE COFFEE CREAMER

1 cup sugar
1/2 cup corn syrup (Don't forget to make the homemade version!)
1/4 cup water
5 oz. evaporated milk (Don't forget to make the homemade version!)
Vanilla
Spices and/or extracts

Bring everything to a boil over medium heat for 2-3 minutes. Remove from heat and add 5 oz. evaporated milk, 2 tsp. vanilla, and 1/2 tsp. cinnamon. You could also use nutmeg, hazelnut or caramel extract, or any other spice that sounds tasty!

CHOCOLATE CARAMEL COFFEE CREAMER

1 cup sugar
1/2 cup corn syrup
1/4 cup plus 2 Tbsp. water
1 1/4 cup unsweetened cocoa
5 oz. evaporated milk

Bring everything to a boil over medium heat for 2-3 minutes. Remove from heat and add 5 oz. evaporated milk, 2 tsp. caramel extract, and 2 tsp. hazelnut extract. Again, you can have fun play around with the extracts and spices. I'd love to hear what else you come up with! Store in a pint jar in the refrigerator for about ten days.

I have found canning instructions for this, but I have not tried it yet. Should you choose to go rouge, the instructions are to use pints in a water bath canner for 60 minutes. Good on the shelf for a year.

MAGIC SHELL HACK!
(Chocolate hardening ice cream topper)

2 cups chocolate chips
1 cup coconut oil

Melt the two in a saucepan on medium heat. Stir well. And you're done. Store in a glass jar or container in the cupboard. If you put it in the fridge, it will harden solid. If it hardens on a cold day in the cupboard, just microwave in 15-second intervals until liquid again. Pour over ice cream and give it 30 seconds or so to harden. You can use any flavor chips with this to create unique ice cream topper flavors.

BROWN SUGAR

When I first found out you could make your own brown sugar, I was blown away.

Cue the Keanu Reeves voice. *No. Way.*

I always wondered what kind of voodoo witchcraft they performed in secret factories to create brown sugar. Come to find out, it's ridiculously easy and costs next to nothing. I have not purchased brown sugar in over four years. I did purchase a gallon of molasses, which, looking back might have been overkill. I still have 2 quarts of that gallon from several years ago. At least I know I won't need any for another two years.

All brown sugar consists of is white sugar and molasses. That. Is. It. Normally, I mix up a batch in my mixer, but my bowl was in the dishwasher so I did it by hand. Here's another thing. I don't measure. Sorry, I just don't. Less molasses will give you light brown sugar. More will give you dark. I started with about 8 cups of sugar and added.... about this much molasses.

Four, maybe five tablespoons if I had to guess. Trust me. It's hard to screw this up. Worst thing that can happen is you'll end up with darker brown sugar than you wanted. (Just add more white sugar if that happens.) Go slowly, adding a few tablespoons at a time. A little goes a long way.

I promise, a few batches from now, you'll be dumping and pouring and mixing without a second thought. Mix it together until it blends. This gets testy at the end so I used a wide wooden spoon and did more of a smearing motion to encourage the little balls of molasses to mix in. Five minutes later, I had this.

CORN SYRUP IS expensive and usually has high fructose involved, which plays havoc with our pancreas worse than plain sugar alone.

Sweetened condensed milk is a staple for baking and holidays but it, too, is expensive. Evaporated milk isn't terribly expensive, but why buy it if you don't have to. Here's how to make all three.

CORN SYRUP

Candy thermometer
2 cups white sugar
3/4 cup water
1/4 tsp. cream of tartar
Pinch of salt

Bring all ingredients to a boil stirring constantly. Reduce heat to a simmer. Cover for three minutes. Uncover and simmer to soft ball stage. Once it reaches soft ball stage, I remove it from the heat and let it cool before transferring into a quart jar. I normally make this only when I need it, but since it's all sugar, it would stay good for quite a long time. Your only worry is crystallization. If it crystallizes, just reheat until the crystals dissolve and use right away. I have made pecan pies with this even though traditionally, pecan pie calls for dark. I suppose if you must have that caramelized color, you could add food coloring or play around with half brown sugar half white sugar.

EVAPORATED MILK

1 1/2 cups water
1 cup instant nonfat milk powder
Shake or blend until combined.

That was hard, wasn't it? If you need it to be "whole" evaporated milk, add 2 Tbsp. oil or melted butter. This will make around 12 oz., but always measure out what you need for the recipe. It is also something I make as needed. (Although I am hunting around for canning options. While it is a milk product, I'm rouge like that.)

SWEETENED CONDENSED MILK

1/2 cup water
1 cup sugar
3 Tbsp. butter
1 cup instant nonfat milk

Bring water, sugar, and butter to a boil. Let cool slightly, and then add 1 cup instant nonfat milk. Whisk smooth. Make one "can" of sweetened condensed milk. Keeps in the fridge for 2 weeks.

I love these recipes because it really illustrates how just a few ingredients can become several different things.

BARBECUE SAUCE

1 cup ketchup
½ cup water
2 Tbsp. apple cider vinegar
1 Tbsp. Worcestershire
1 Tbsp. molasses
1 tsp. garlic salt

Mix all ingredients in a saucepan, heat over medium heat for 15 minutes to blend seasonings. Let cool. Use right away or store in the refrigerator for one week.

AU JUS

I never, ever buy Au Jus anymore. It's so ridiculously easy to make. If I had to put a price on making this, I'd say a nickel at most.

2 cups water
1 Tbsp. beef bouillon granules
¼ tsp. pepper
¼ tsp. crushed red pepper flakes
¼ tsp. garlic salt
(optional) ¼ tsp. seasoned salt

Mix all in a saucepan, bring to a boil, and serve. Perfect for French dips!

PIZZA SAUCE

1 15ox can tomato sauce
1 6 oz. can tomato paste
1 Tbsp. oregano
Dash garlic
1 Tbsp. sugar

Mix all ingredients over medium heat. If you have time, let it simmer for an hour or so to let the flavors really meld together. If you're short on time, this can be used right away. Store leftovers in the refrigerator for three days.

RED PEPPER RELISH

I REMEMBER EATING this as far back as I can recall. It was always on the appetizer tray in restaurants, every older person's house I went to had it in jelly jars on the table at mealtime, and I was witness to more than one act of thievery. I think it's a Yankee thing, this Pepper Relish, as I've always known it to be called—but maybe not—maybe the whole country has caught on to it by now. I just know the sweet and spicy-at-the-same-time flavor is unique, and once I tasted it as a child, I was forever left wanting more. I know that people eat it on meat and on sandwiches, and its greatest popularity is in being eaten mixed with cream cheese on crackers. Always served room temperature, never cold. I guess there is no wrong way to eat it. My favorite? Just out of the jar. All by itself. Like you would a cranberry sauce with turkey and stuffing.

Keeps 6 MONTHS in the refrigerator. Take out what you want to serve and allow it to reach room temperature before serving.

1 ½ lbs. tomatoes
⅓-½ cup oil
1 ⅔ cups onions, measure after chopping. (Finely chop)
1 ¾ cups sweet red peppers (Chopped medium fine)
1 ½ cups red wine vinegar
1 ½ cups sugar
1 cup golden raisins
2 cloves garlic, minced
½ tsp. salt
¼ tsp. black pepper

⅛ tsp. allspice
2 small dried red chili peppers—chopped
1 tsp. ground ginger

Peel tomatoes by dropping them in boiling water for a moment then placing them in cold water. Remove skins and chop tomatoes. Puree tomatoes and press through sieve extracting all of the liquid. Discard the pulp. (Don't throw it away. It's great in soup or spaghetti sauce)

Heat olive oil in heavy pan over med-low heat. Add in onions and cook 8-10 minutes to brown. Add red peppers and stir, reduce heat, cover and cook on low for 10 minutes. Add vinegar and bring to a simmer. Simmer uncovered until vinegar is reduced by half… about 20-30 minutes.

Add tomatoes to the pepper mixture now, and 1 cup of sugar then add raisins, garlic, ginger, salt, pepper, allspice, and chili peppers. Cover and cook for 1 hour.

Uncover and continue cooking until relish thickens to spreadable consistency. Up to 2 hours. **Taste at this point, and add additional ½ cup sugar** IF NEEDED. Ladle into clean jars, let cool and cover. Refrigerate for up to 6 months.

BONUS RECIPES

EASY CHEESE SAUCE

1 can cream of mushroom soup
1 8 oz. container sour cream
1 cup shredded cheddar cheese

Combine all ingredients in a saucepan and mix well. Heat on medium until melted. Do not boil. Use for topping vegetables, casseroles or as a dip.

SIMPLE FUDGE

1 12 oz. package chocolate chips
1 14 oz. can sweetened condensed milk (make your own)
1 tsp. vanilla

Combine chocolate chips and milk in a glass dish and microwave on high for three minutes. Stir until blended. Add vanilla, stir, and then pour into 8-inch buttered dish. Chill until firm. Cut into squares and get ready to make more. This will go fast! You can substitute peanut butter or mint chips for variety as well.

A BASIC LIME/HONEY SALAD DRESSING

1/4 cup lime juice

1/4 cup honey

1/4 -1/2 tsp. Dijon mustard

(You can substitute for regular mustard, adjusting to taste)

Mix all ingredients together. Cover and refrigerate. Serve cold over vegetable or fruit salads.

PINEAPPLE TEA

1 46 oz. can pineapple juice

2 packages inexpensive iced mochas

1 qt. coffee (brewed to taste from mild to strong)

1 qt. chocolate milk (make your own chocolate sauce to keep costs down)

Mix together and store in the fridge. I like to use very strong brewed coffee over instant. There's a better flavor. And I use just enough chocolate in the milk to have the mocha flavor but not overpower the coffee. I have added 2 tsp. of caramel extract and another time hazelnut extract and liked it.

TV DINNERS

MAKING MY OWN TV dinners is something I love to do. It not only uses my leftovers in a great way, it saves refrigerator space, money, and time, and it gives me great meals without cooking. Making my own TV dinners is the best way to ensure that my leftovers don't get wasted. We all know how easily things are overlooked in the fridge or pushed to the back and forgotten. The next thing we know, something that was delicious last time we saw it is now unrecognizable and has to be thrown away. MYO TV dinners and getting them into the freezer the same day you make that meal prevents that waste. Some idea for MYO TV dinners include:

Meatballs and sauce

Add a roll and mozzarella cheese and you have a meatball sandwich. Simply heat the meatballs and sauce, put on roll, add cheese, and slip in the oven for 5-10 minutes until cheese melts.

Chicken Dinner

Freeze an entire meal together. Chicken, stuffing, potatoes, gravy, and biscuit. Put it all in a zip type bag or vacuum bag, seal and freeze.

Pasta dishes

Anything with spaghetti sauce in it will taste better after being frozen. Just be careful about overcooking your pasta. It tends to get mushy when it's frozen. Cook it to *al dente*.

Stuffed Peppers/Stuffed Cabbage

Wonderful dishes for this!

Mac and cheese with chicken tenders

Corn Fritters and Pork Medallions

Great TV dinner and you won't find that in the grocery store! Reheat in oven at 400.

MOST THINGS THAT I cook, I make into TV dinners with my food saver vacuum sealer. I don't reheat in the microwave. I use my oven. I thaw in the fridge, then cut the bags open, slide the contents into a pan I've sprayed with cooking spray. Reheating at 400 degrees makes the food taste as if it was just prepared. It's crisp and hot. Nothing is soggy, tough, and dry or tastes off.

I try to think about how long before I may use something, and that helps me determine how I will store it in my freezer. If it's something I know that I will use pretty soon, I use some foil and a zip bag. If I plan on saving it longer, I use the vacuum sealer bags. It's more cost effective that way. The vacuum sealer bags cost a lot for short-term storage. Some people wash and reuse the food saver bags. I'm not comfortable doing that when raw meat is involved. I live a frugal life, but I'm not there yet.

**Molly's two cents on making TV dinners. I buy glass pie plates at the thrift store for a dollar a piece. I place the meals in those and cover tightly with foil and label. Then reheat in the oven.

CHEEZ WHIZ

DO YOU REMEMBER Cheez Whiz? Do you remember Cheez Whiz sandwiches on white bread? When you were a kid, your mom would make you this sandwich with a thick layer of gooey, bright orange cheese spread during summer vacation, and it just made everything so good! The sun was brighter, the pool was cooler, the boy next door was...well…. Cheez Whiz…..great stuff! It's really hard to find these days, so I figured out how to make some the other night and gave another thought to that boy next door from that summer…

About ¾ cup milk
About 3 "inches" of the small block of Velveeta cheese

I didn't measure, but it came out perfectly. Just right for spreading after being refrigerated. Heat the milk on the stove as you're cutting the cheese into small cubes. Drop the cubes into the milk and stir. Stir often to keep from sticking. When all the cheese has melted, pour into jar or plastic container with lid. When cool, it's ready to enjoy. Makes about 1-1 ¼ cups. Refrigerate.

SEASONING MIXES

SEASONINGS GIVE FOODS that are already good, great flavors. I discovered how to use several new spices and herbs a few years ago, believe it or not—by scent. I bought several new fragrant jars, and then as I prepared different foods, I opened them and decided by their aroma, whether or not each had a place in whatever I was cooking. This method worked perfectly for me! My nose told me just as accurately as any chef could have that sage would be amazing on pork. And that dill weed is delicious in potato salad.

So, use your nose—if you're not so informed about spices, like me. And ALWAYS experiment. There are many seasoning mixes out there now, and they're pretty expensive. Most of us have the basics on hand to prepare them ourselves, saving that cost. I use all of these regularly and love them. All you need is a bowl, empty spice jar, and a funnel.

THIS CAJUN SEASONING is a great way to flavor up plain, white rice. You can either stir in 1 tsp. Cajun seasoning per cup of cooked rice with a little oil or butter or sprinkle on your white rice to suit individual tastes.

It also makes a great dry rub for meats, poultry, and fish before cooking. Simply rub on both sides of the meat, let rest 10 minutes, and then cook.

Sprinkle on buttered popcorn for a real treat!

I use it the most on fried potatoes.

CAJUN SEASONING

½ Tbsp. thyme

1 Tbsp. paprika

1 Tbsp. cayenne pepper

1 Tbsp. oregano

½ Tbsp. onion powder

1 Tbsp. garlic powder

½ Tbsp. black pepper

2 ½ Tbsp. salt

Measure and stir all seasonings together in a small bowl then use a funnel to pour the mixture into a seasoning jar with a sprinkle top.

THIS SEASONING MIXTURE is another choice for a meat rub. It's my favorite for pork but works equally well on chicken and beef. It is the perfect blend of spicy and sweet. I bet it'll have you licking your fingers… Forget Colonel "Whatshisname…"

JAMAICAN SEASONING

1 tsp. Allspice

½ tsp. paprika

½ tsp. red pepper flakes

½ tsp. nutmeg

½ tsp. chives

¼ tsp. thyme

¼ tsp. cloves

½ tsp. ground ginger

¼ tsp. cinnamon

1 tsp. brown sugar dark or light

1 tsp. garlic powder

1 Tbsp. salt

½ tsp. black pepper

1 tsp. onion powder

Mix all seasonings together in a bowl then pour into an airtight jar or container. Use as a rub for meat or fish. Also can be used to season vegetables when you roast or grill them. And the same way as the Cajun Seasoning above, in rice.

WIDELY USED IN not only Asian cooking but other cuisines too, Chinese 5 Spice is a mixture of fragrant, wonderful spices that lend heat and sweet to many dishes, but it's especially good on meats. Its price can be off-putting, so, if you already have a stocked seasoning supply, you are going to be happy to know, this recipe won't cost you much, maybe nothing...but you'll reap tons of flavor.

CHINESE 5 SPICE

3 Tbsp. cinnamon

6 stars anise or 2 tsp. anise seeds

1 ½ tsp. fennel seeds

1 ½ tsp. whole black peppercorns

¾ tsp. ground cloves

Combine all ingredients in blender or food mill and blend until finely ground. Store in airtight container and use within 2 months for best flavors. Makes ¼ cup.

SIMPLE SAUSAGE SEASONING

THIS SEASONING MIX can turn ground beef or pork—even ground chicken or turkey into breakfast sausage. Well, breakfast sausage flavored beef... and *breakfast sausage flavored* is good enough if you're out of sausage. Turn your ground beef into sausage for spur-of-the-moment "breakfast for dinner." Add some scrambled eggs and Molly's biscuits, drizzled with some of her MYO maple syrup, and done! I'm sure you'll find many uses for this. If you prefer, you can add fennel seeds as well. I don't like them.

1 Tbsp. sage
¼ cup plus ¼ tsp. black pepper
¼ Tbsp. nutmeg
¼ Tbsp. salt

Stir all ingredients together in a jar and keep dry. Mix 1 ¼ Tbsp. of this mixture to one pound of ground beef, pork, chicken, or turkey before cooking.

TACO SEASONING

1/4 C. plus 1 Tbsp. chili powder

1 1/4 tsp. garlic powder

1 1/4 tsp. onion powder

1 1/4 tsp. crushed red pepper flakes

1 1/4 tsp. oregano

2 1/2 tsp. paprika

2 Tbsp. plus 1 1/2 tsp. ground cumin

1 Tbsp. salt

1 Tbsp. black pepper

Mix together and store in an airtight jar. For every pound of ground beef, use two tablespoons of spice mix.

BEEF STEW SEASONING MIX

1 cup all-purpose flour

2 teaspoons dried oregano

1 Tbsp. dried basil

1 tsp. dried rosemary

1 Tbsp. dried parsley

1 Tbsp. salt

2 tablespoons black pepper

2 tablespoons paprika

1/2 tsp. cayenne pepper

1 Tbsp. celery seed

2 tablespoons onion powder

Mix well and store in an airtight container. Use 3 Tbsp. mix per pound of stew meat.

SHAKE AND BAKE

4 cups flour
4 cups soda crackers, crushed
4 Tbsp. salt
2 Tbsp. sugar
2 tsp. garlic powder
2 tsp. onion powder
3 Tbsp. paprika
1/4 cup vegetable oil

Mix well and store indefinitely in the refrigerator in a covered container. Moisten the chicken pieces with milk or water, then shake dry.

Pour about 2 cups mixture, or more if needed, into a plastic bag. Place chicken pieces, one at a time, in the bag and shake until evenly coated. Bake coated chicken pieces in a greased shallow pan at 375 degrees for 45-60 minutes. Discard plastic bag with unused coating. DO NOT reuse extra coating that has come into contact with raw chicken!

POULTRY SEASONING

2 tsp. sage
1 1/2 tsp. thyme
1 tsp. marjoram
3/4 tsp. rosemary
1/2 tsp. nutmeg

1/2 tsp. black pepper

Mix well. Rub poultry seasoning on the outside of the chicken before roasting. This homemade seasoning can also be used in stuffing and in soups.

BEFORE I STARTED making this, I hated the crap in the stores, other than the really pricey blue cheese dressing they keep in the cold produce section. You know the stuff. But I couldn't afford that. I started making this, and no other dressing would compare. So fresh, such a difference.

You definitely have to make it at least 30 minutes before you want to eat it though… or more. Now, my local store is selling that pricey stuff, buy two, get three free... so I haven't made this in a while, but who knows? If they stop that sale, I'll be making my own again…. or if *GASP!*—I run out.

I love this recipe because it doesn't require sour cream, something I rarely have on hand because I don't have a car, and it always spoils on me before I use it. The ingredients are all staple items, which means I can always make Blue Cheese Dressing this way.

BLUE CHEESE DRESSING

½ cup mayo
¼ cup milk
1 tsp. vinegar
½ tsp. lemon juice
½ tsp. fresh garlic—(or garlic powder)
1 Tbsp. oil

Blue Cheese Crumbles—¼ lb. or whatever suits you.
(I always add more!)

Mix all ingredients together and refrigerate for ½ hour before serving.

I MAKE THESE sweet pickles every year. I started my first year on my own. I love the scent of the pickling spice, the Zen-ness of working with my hands and seeing the jars line up as I work. It's the same feeling I get when I make bread too. That feeling that I'm doing something that generations before me have done...or that maybe I did, in another lifetime. It doesn't matter to me whether I'm preparing bread or pickles—what matters is that I'm preparing food to put up for another day. Creating...security? That's a good feeling.

I'll soon be making them again, and I'm especially excited this year because I *grew* my own cucumbers! Just one plant, in a container, but I have enough cukes for me.

These pickles are super crunchy and easy. Go beg, borrow and steal some jars—ANY jars and make some. They last 9 months in the fridge.

REFRIGERATOR SWEET PICKLES

Wash and cut pickling cucumbers s into ¼ inch slices.
Mix:
4 cups vinegar
4 cups sugar
¼ tsp. salt
3 Tbsp. pickling spice

Dash of cloves
Dash of cinnamon

Mix ingredients in pot and bring to a boil. Let cool. Fill jars with slices of cucumbers. Pour cooled mixture over top of cukes in jars, all the way up. Put tops on and refrigerate. (You can add in slices of other veggies if you'd like as well...onions are good and beets too.)

DILL PICKLES

3 ½ cups water
1 Tbsp. sugar
1 ¼ cups vinegar
1 Tbsp. sea salt
3 cloves garlic
4 cups pickling cucumber spears
2 heads fresh dill

Stir water, vinegar, sugar, and salt together in pan on high. Boil. Remove from heat and cool. Combine cuke spears, dill, and garlic in jars—pour vinegar mixture in to cover. Refrigerate. Keeps 3 months in refrigerator. You can eliminate the garlic if you wish.

IF THE BOTTOM FALLS OUT

Molly

What to do when the bottom falls out.

OF ALL THE monthly bills you or I have, the most flexible one is the grocery bill. Things like rent, car, insurance, etc. are mostly fixed. If something catastrophic were to happen to our finances, such as one of us completely losing our income, instead of panicking and acting out of fear, here's what I'd do.

First, evaluate every bill. I'd tally up what money was projected to come and what bills were going out for the next few months. This will show me where I need to shore things up and by how much. I would look at and rid myself of every expense not needed for living. Cable—gone. Subscriptions like Hulu, Netflix, etc.—gone. I'd look at my Internet, too and see if I can find it cheaper somewhere else. Because the Internet is used for job searches and learning, I'd say it's actually higher on the priority list. That said, I'm sure there is a library nearby and with a library comes free use of the Internet—if it comes down to it.

Cell phones need a hard look, too. Most people are wrapped up in an expensive plan. That needs to be reduced to the least expensive option possible, even if that means downgrading phones and having talk and text only. There are a lot of inexpensive options out there now. I need to stay in touch and communicate. I do not 'need' to stream Netflix and Snapchat and

Facebook. I can hear the moaning and groaning now. It is so easy to feel like we can't live without certain technology when, in fact, we lived quite well without all this stuff just twenty years ago. Trust me, mankind, you will survive (perhaps thrive) with a downgraded phone and no data. You cannot eat data. Nor will data keep you warm in the winter.

My gym membership would go. Exercise can and, for centuries did, happen outside a gym.

Areas of the budget such as clothing and entertainment are gone. I'd start making my boys underwear. Okay, I'm just kidding. Though, I do know how to make very nice linen boxers, I wouldn't jump to that just yet. I would, however, threaten to make them out of a floral print flour sack if they gave me any guff about the cable.

I'd call the bank to see if there is an option to "skip a payment" on the car loan. Lots of loans have this feature built in, and I've read most people use it for the month of December go figure.) I'd use it now to provide a cushion. Most insurance companies don't have this feature, but I'd call to see what the absolute rock bottom rates I can get are. I would, however, keep roadside assistance. Mine runs $5 a month—Murphy's Law and all.

I'd drop to liability only on my paid for vehicles and check my financed one to shave off every dime possible from that policy.

I am on an equal payment plan with the utilities, but if I weren't, I'd hop on in a hurry. This makes budgeting easier as the bill stays the same. It also means my gas bill won't get uglier and uglier as we get into winter.

I'd look at what I "do" that can be monetized. It wouldn't be writing, either. It can take up to a year or longer to get a book out. I do love woodworking, and I can make furniture. The quickest and easiest thing would be a pioneer style twin bed frame that I could make for about $25 and sell for at least $100.

What talents or hobbies do you have that you could monetize in a hurry if you put your back into it?

After I'd gone through every single expense and determined what we can live without and then mercilessly cut those things from our life, I'd look at food. I'd make a one-week menu for all meals and snacks. I'd make sure they were inexpensive meals too, breaking that down into basic ingredients. I'd mark off what we already had and make a grocery list for what was left. We would, for the duration of the financial emergency, have a one-week menu that I'd use the whole month.

If it looked like our emergency was going to be a long-term one, I'd look at what I had in the attic, basement, or storage unit that could be liquidated. I'd look at the car and the house. Could we live with one car? If I rented, I'd start keeping my eyes out for more inexpensive housing. If I owned, I'd contact the bank, explain what was happening, and see to what degree they could work with me. I would consider selling if it meant I would receive a financial buffer (hence, protecting against eventual foreclosure) and get into a less expensive housing situation to better weather the storm.

If all of this weren't enough, I'd look at severely downsizing to tiny living. With tiny living come tiny bills. I've actually done this, and I'm still dreaming about doing it again. Our tiny house was a motor home. We did it to save for a dream we have to buy land and homestead. We were able to save just over ten thousand dollars in five months. Utah has been a longer than intended pit stop on our journey, but my point is, our tiny living was by choice, and we had a lot of fun. My youngest told me it was the best six months of his childhood. Four people and four cats in 280-sq. feet. Yet it was the best times he can remember.

While the boys had fun with woods to traipse through, campfires, fort building and homemade flaming arrows, my experience was mostly good. It was stressful on occasion. (Like when one of the flaming arrows flew right past the R.V. with propane on board)

I could clean top to bottom in fifteen minutes but it only took five to mess up again. Yes, at times we got tired of bumping into each other. But we learned how to live together, and I'd venture to say the boys got along better then than they do now with ten times the room. We definitely did more as a family than we do now.

If you decide to go this route, you can either sink money into a stick-built tiny home on a trailer frame or find motorhomes, fifth wheels and campers inexpensively, used. Update the interior (make it home) to whatever your budget will allow. Find a nice, clean, family friendly campground and check out the "Fulltime Families" links on YouTube and the Internet. The movement to ditch the stranglehold of a mortgage and live free (relatively speaking) is really catching on. Even if finances force you to consider this option, it can still be a *conscious choice*. Turn a disaster into an adventure. It really is all about the attitude and the approach. Embarking on tiny living as a proactive means to weather the storm or get ahead can be fantastic, empowering, and memorable if you want it to be.

If you have the attitude, "Oh, my goodness, we've lost everything. Now we're homeless and living at a campground or someone's backyard, how did we fall so low?" I wouldn't plan on it being a family bonding experience.

Not panicking when the bottom falls out is vital. Remain in control and be proactive. Cut the cable bill long before they cut the electric off. It's really common sense. Come up with a short term, medium term, and long-term plan. Prepare your family for what the medium-term and long-term plan might look like. Moving in with family? Renting out the house while you live somewhere cheaper? A motorhome or fifth wheel and nightly roasting of marshmallows listening to the crickets? (I'll vote that one every time.) Moving to a state with job prospects and a better economy?

I realize I've gotten into worst-case scenarios here. It won't be like that for everyone. But for those whose bump in the road turns into an all-out financial storm, stay calm, stay in control, and ***do not worry*** about what anyone else says or thinks about the choices you have to make to take care of yourself and your family.

Daisy

Molly's opener "what to do when the bottom falls out" is filled with thoughtful insight, and more than a little of it has been put to the test with the life events that her family has endured. I would be inclined to take her advice.

I'm a preventative type gal. In the time I've been on my own, I've learned not to give Murphy and his merry band of laws the chance to mess with me, to borrow from Molly's description of what she'd do if the bottom fell out of her life. I pared my phone and cable bill down to the lowest possible amounts and services. I was the only person I knew that didn't have texting or Internet on my phone for about two and a half years or so. I was determined to make being independent work. Cable TV and texting were things I could live without. I weighed each purchase, each expense, and made decisions based on not only their financial value, but also their worth in my life. Different things matter to different people. Everyone's priorities are not the same.

Not having a car, and there being no public transportation in my town, made getting around very difficult then, as it still does. My apartment being on the outskirts of the village meant that everything was just about a mile away. Pharmacy, laundry mat, convenience store, etc. Grocery store is another mile or so from there. So the decision to rent-to-own a stackable washer and dryer was one that I struggled with for a bit, and then made out of necessity. It was a huge chunk of my budget to make those payments monthly for twenty-four months, but I sacrificed a lot of things to do it. It was easier than dragging my laundry down the stairs from a second-floor apartment, trying to get a ride to the laundry mat, be there for at least two hours a week, spending the fifteen dollars a week at the laundry mat, and then drag the laundry back up the stairs. I weighed that out, especially for the wintertime, and to me—the cost of the washer and dryer and their convenience were worth the sacrifices I made to have them. There were many. I had no extra money at all. I celebrated the last payment like it was my twenty-first birthday. It was a great feeling and a great accomplishment. I paid for those appliances MYSELF.

Still, as Molly says, we all have the same basic needs for food, clothing and shelter. Beyond that, everything else can be negotiated. I still have basic cable, but now I have texting on my phone since my provider now has a much cheaper plan that includes unlimited texting, Internet, and calling for less than I used to pay for just a limited number of minutes per month. I do not have a house phone, only a cell, as I need a cell for health reasons anyhow—so why have a house phone, too? Don't need it. No car means no car expenses. Perfect. I spend a little money every month on supplies for my creative pursuits. I'm very thrifty with that. I repurpose furniture and other cast-off items. I try to reuse things I already have in keeping with the frugal lifestyle. I also paint with acrylic paints on canvas panels, so every few months, I restock those things a little at a time. I sew and crochet, do decoupage, journal, papier-mâché, upcycle clothing, and I read like crazy. I can't spend a lot of money on the things I enjoy, and I don't. That's another book altogether.

I have plans to buy a tiny house and be fully independent. Ever since I saw my first tiny house, it's been my dream. I'll get there.

So, when the bottom falls out, as Molly says... I plan to already be somewhere in my tiny house, tending my garden, reading books and writing more books, and eating good, frugal food.

MEASUREMENT GUIDE

A handy measurement guide for buying bulk foods.

ONE POUND OF — EQUALS

Flour — 4 cups

Sugar — 2 cups

Powdered sugar — 3 1/2 cups

Brown sugar — 2 1/4 cups

Molasses — 1 1/3 cups

Butter — 2 cups

Grated cheese — 4 cups

Oatmeal — 6 1/2 cups

OOPSIE BREAD RECIPE

The **Oopsie Bread recipe that's been shared thousands of times!!**

Oopsie!! This is what I use for "bread" when I'm restricting carbs. For months, I made homemade bread for the family and made this for myself to use. It isn't really bread at all and has no flour or sugar, but it holds up well to all kinds of sandwiches and for soft tacos. Hubby loves it on or off low carb. The boys are getting used to it. It has a slight egg flavor if eaten alone, but I've noticed it takes on the flavor of what's on the sandwich. I highly recommend peanut butter and sugar-free raspberry jam.

OOPSIE BREAD

3 eggs
1/2 cup cream cheese
pinch of salt
1/2 tsp. baking powder

Separate eggs. Whip the egg whites until stiff. Mix the yolks and the cream cheese together until smooth. Add baking powder. Fold cream cheese mixture into egg whites. Mix well but gently. Pour onto parchment paper and spread thin. Bake at 350 for 25 minutes. After it cools, cut it into 6 or 8 slices depending on how big you like sandwiches.

NON FOOD FRUGALITY

Do you have a dirty grill or oven rack?

Did you know it'll come sparkling clean with no chemicals?

Just use balled up aluminum foil that's been gently used, to lightly scrub, then rinse!

Discolored or dirty looking white kitchen appliances?

Mix 50% white vinegar with 50% water in a spray bottle. Spray your appliances and wipe clean, they will be shiny white! The vinegar smell will dissipate in moments.

Do you have a pan with burnt on, stuck on food?
A baking dish even?

Wet it with water, sprinkle the burnt on areas with baking soda, let sit 15 minutes and wash normally. For regular use, I keep an old seasoning bottle that I washed out, filled with baking soda on my kitchen sink. It works perfectly for sprinkling and the top keeps it from getting moisture inside.

No more soaking pans overnight or for hours.

Leftover Tomato juice or V8 Juice??

Pour it into ice cube trays and freeze into cubes, then dump the cubes into a zip-top bag and keep in your freezer door. The next time you're making tacos, chili, spaghetti sauce, sloppy joes, Spanish rice, etc....grab a cube or two for extra flavor. I bet you can think of other uses for them....deglazing pans...? You bet! I've done it.

Do you make bread or rolls?

Save your butter wrappers and use them to wipe butter onto your bread and rolls when they come out of the oven. You would be surprised to know that there's enough butter on one wrapper to do several rolls.

Do you have a "Bacon Drippins" jar? You should!

After cooking bacon, let your pan drippings—drippins', lol—cool then pour them into a jar, unstrained and unfiltered. Use these drippings to fry eggs in, to grease bread pans, to top cornbread before it cooks, to grease your waffle iron, and more. Add that yummy bacon flavor to all kinds of things in your kitchen… share the bacon love.

RECYCLING: MAKING SOMETHING OLD, NEW AGAIN

My life is frugal, not just my eating. Anything I can reuse or make into something else, rather than send it to the landfill, I do. Not just for frugality, but for the sake of our planet's future. Here I took two chairs that I no longer used and made a bench—not the same way that everyone else does—I faced mine toward each other and cut the backs lower. I often see upcycling projects online, but I don't copy them. I use them to inspire my own ideas.

INEXPENSIVE CAKE STANDS.

THIS ONE FALLS under the category, "Why didn't I think of this before?" Recently, I was at a craft show and came across a woman selling beautiful cake stands. They weren't the crystal clear or white kinds you buy in the store. With unique colors and styles, some were single tier, some multi-tier... I was in awe. When I looked closer, I realized these were actually just dishes glued together. This is such a simple, obvious idea, yet it never crossed my mind. (Even though I LOVE cake stands) For holidays, I love to have all the desserts arranged on different dishes, sitting at different levels, and sprinkle candles or oil lamps throughout. Until now, I've simply slipped things under the tablecloth like a few books, a small parcel box or a casserole dish, anything to give that elegant buffet look.

Now, looking and doing are two different things. There have been a few times I've seen something in the store and tried to recreate it at home only to struggle. But this is so simple, I was fairly certain I could handle it. You can use dishes, platters, saucers, or chargers. For the base, you can use bowls, dessert dishes, wine glasses, vases, figurines—the list goes on and on.

I went to the thrift store and spent five dollars (plus another two dollars for super glue.) I made three cake stands, two of which match. It was silly how excited I was doing this. Now I can create stands that match my kitchen, my personality, and even make themed ones for holidays, birthdays, Easter, weddings, multi-tiered, Halloween, personalize for friends and family as gifts... The possibilities are endless. By the time I'm done, I may have to build a second hutch just to hold all my cake stands!

ABOUT THE AUTHORS

Daisy Lynn is an artist who lives in New York. Creating is who she is, not what she does.

When she's not painting on canvas or hardwood, she can be found putting a coat of paint on some forgotten-by-the-roadside piece of furniture. A self-proclaimed Junk Gypsy, Daisy has repurposed several pieces of wood furniture into new, useable and beautiful creations. When asked which she prefers now, painting or upcycling furniture, it takes her a moment to answer. Painting was where her creativity was born, and it opened her to express herself creatively in all areas.

Daisy is the mother of grown children. She has used that inborn creativity in her kitchen through the years of their growing up. Money was tight, but the kids were never hungry, despite Daisy being disabled when they were pretty young.

Daisy learned to shop and meal plan and to really live frugally four years ago when she exited an abusive marriage. Having no money and no choices made her have to return to her abusive husband four times. The fifth time she left, she vowed would be her last. She knew she'd have to do something different in order to remain free this time.

Now on her own, Daisy uses that creativity in the kitchen again, making her own foods, writing her own recipes, and reusing leftovers in ways that are delicious! What's equally important to her is teaching others how to do this too. It just takes a little creativity.

M. L. Gardner is the bestselling author of the *1929* series. Gardner is frugal to a fault, preserving the old ways of living by canning, cooking from scratch, and woodworking. Nostalgic stories from her grandmother's life during the Great Depression inspired Gardner to write the *1929* series—as well as her own research into the Roarin' Twenties. She has authored eight books, two novellas, and one book of short stories. Gardner is married with three kids and four cats. She resides in northern Utah.

www.mlgardnerbooks.com

Made in United States
Troutdale, OR
05/08/2025

31181728R00129